YoungWriters 2006 Poetry Competition for 11-

"I have a dream that my four children will one day live in a nation where they will not be judged by the color of their skin, but by the content of their character."

Martin Luther King

I have a dream

words to change the world

- MOTIVATE your pupils to write and appreciate poetry.
- INSPIRE them to share their hopes and dreams for the future.
- BOOST awareness of your school's creative ability.
- WORK alongside the National Curriculum or the high level National Qualification Skills.
- Supports the *Every Child Matters - Make a Positive Contribution* outcome.
- Over £7,000 of great prizes for schools and pupils.

"When I was out there I was never ever alone, there was always a team of people behind me, in mind if not in body."
Ellen MacArthur

Southern England Vol II
Edited by Claire Tupholme

 Young**Writers**

First published in Great Britain in 2006 by:
Young Writers
Remus House
Coltsfoot Drive
Peterborough
PE2 9JX
Telephone: 01733 890066
Website: www.youngwriters.co.uk

SB ISBN 1 84602 652 0

Foreword

Imagine a teenager's brain; a fertile yet fragile expanse teeming with ideas, aspirations, questions and emotions. Imagine a classroom full of racing minds, scratching pens writing an endless stream of ideas and thoughts . . .

. . . Imagine your words in print reaching a wider audience. Imagine that maybe, just maybe, your words can make a difference. Strike a chord. Touch a life. Change the world. Imagine no more . . .

'I Have a Dream' is a series of poetry collections written by 11 to 18-year-olds from schools and colleges across the UK and overseas. Pupils were invited to send us their poems using the theme 'I Have a Dream'. Selected entries range from dreams they've experienced to childhood fantasies of stardom and wealth, through inspirational poems of their dreams for a better future and of people who have influenced and inspired their lives.

The series is a snapshot of who and what inspires, influences and enthuses young adults of today. It shows an insight into their hopes, dreams and aspirations of the future and displays how their dreams are an escape from the pressures of today's modern life. Young Writers are proud to present this anthology, which is truly inspired and sure to be an inspiration to all who read it.

Contents

Amy Langley (13)	87
Reece Ellis (13)	88
Nicola Dimbleby (14)	89
James Casbolt (13)	90
Steven Marr (13)	91
Aqeel Rafiq (13)	92
Grace Claxton (11)	93
Connor Iontton (14)	94
Luke Brown (13)	95
Ericha Stephanie Antonio (13)	96
Matthew Arrowsmith (14)	97
Marcus Wan (12)	98
Amy Owen (13)	98
Lauren Davies (13)	99
Dami Oloyede (13)	100
Abby Brealey (13)	101
Amy Boswell (14)	102
Lauren Everett (13)	103
Katie Ellingworth (13)	104

Lycée Francais Charles de Gaulle, London

Celine James (12)	104
Omar Zaghouani (12)	105
Christian Kendrick-Brajou (11)	105
Henry Blake (11)	106
Benjamin Gowie (13)	107
Edward Noakes (12)	108
Claire Bate Roullin (12)	108
Alexander Blakoe (11)	109
Thierry Serafin Nadeau (11)	109
Yannick Moxon (12)	110
Maud de Rohan Willner (12)	110
Francis Jackson (13)	111
Alexandra Lochead (12)	111
Marie-Armance Renaud (12)	112
Jack George (11)	113
Kinvara Jenkins (14)	114
Marie de Noblet (12)	114
Natacha Zouein (12)	115
Benjamin Sagnier (12)	115
Alexandra Sentuc (11)	116

The Poems

I Have A Dream

I have a dream when I grow up
For people to fly.
When I walk outside
For people to be free, not hide.

I have a vision
To be the ignition
Of our beautiful planet
And help everyone.

I have my future generations
To keep alive,
Because I want to be
One to survive.

That was me
Saying to you,
I want to be
Just like glue,
Hold the world together
To make sure we don't rip like leather.

It's cool now
But for the future
I hope it's like I wrote,
Together we can change the future
To be what we want it to be.

Latisha Wright (12)
Capital City Academy, Willesden

That Is My Dream

A poem . . .
There is conflict in the world but we all want peace
We are disgusted by immorality yet it happens
There is terrorism in the world but we all want justice
There is racism in the world yet we are all humans
We all want to be understood yet there is stereotyping
There is civil war between countrymen. But they come from the
                                        same country.
So why, I ask, why does this happen?
Judgement day draws near and only one thing remains: when
                                        will it happen?

In my world -
The boy who blew himself up - was he Shaheed fighting in the way
of Allah, fighting for his country or thought of as nothing but a
                                        bloodthirsty terrorist?
Day and night there are bombs exploding
A world obsessed with nuclear energy and power
What is it with power that makes a brother turn against brother . . . ?
Why do they crave it so? Is it the thrill? Is it the knowledge - which
                                        they know of nothing?

A mother kills her child
A father leaves a home . . .
A mother screams for her lost baby, her lost child
Why does this happen?
That here in this country we have peace,
July - it is summer and bombs explode - we are shocked, the people
                                        are shocked,
But we do not realise that somewhere in this world every second
                                        a bomb explodes

Someone is dead
And not in this world anymore . . .
We turn a blind eye to it.
'It's not my fault, is it?
It's some problem they have in their own country . . .'
We have refugees, moving from one country to another
They are met with hostility.
'They are not one of our own - scum sent from another country'
Half a century ago, a man drops a bomb
When asked how he felt at his destruction

'I was just doing my job . . .'
What is it about orders - which we find so hard to ignore?
We are compelled to obey them whether good or bad.
The politician says he was lied to about the blood in Iraq, said he
                                                    was wrongly led
But he supported the cruelty, the deaths, the grief, the cries, the pain
So what is the point now in speaking out?
They talk about freedom of speech - being able to speak out
                                            against something
It is an abuse of freedom of speech to waste it by drawing cartoons
Why not spend your freedom on speaking out against that which
                                            is bad in the world?
That is my dream
That someday someone will come into this world to free it from its pain.

Amina Seylani (12)
Capital City Academy, Willesden

I Have A Dream

I have a dream cars did not exist,
no more letting off polluted mist.

I have a dream global warming would end,
dying nature we would defend.

I have a dream animals would not become extinct,
the animal population would rise not sink.

I have a dream recycling would make the world better,
because we are the role setters.

I have a dream the world was a healthier place,
filled with sanitary space.

I have a dream the planet was a perfect place,
but we must set an example for the human race.

I have a dream, do you have a dream?

Diamond Abdirahim (12)
Capital City Academy, Willesden

I Have A Dream

A dream of a good lifestyle
So I would never scream
My dream is to have a lot of scenes
What could fall out of my future
To have a fancy car or get richer
I do not know what's going to happen in the future
I want my dream to come true
I have to listen to the teacher
I always said whatever
I could just be a dreamer
My ambition is to be a footballer
Trying to get richer
I'm not thinking about being a goalkeeper
To make a successful future
I have to set aims and goals till I'm older.

Muhamad Hariz Rosli (15)
Capital City Academy, Willesden

I Have A Dream . . .

I magine

H aving an
A nti-
V iolence
E arth

A nti-

D omineers (bullies)
R esulting
E ventually in
A nti-
M isanthropy (hatred).

Zarina Ahmed (12)
Capital City Academy, Willesden

I Had A Dream

I had a dream that I will be running for England in the Olympics 2012.
I had a dream that I had everything that I ever wanted.
I had a dream that I was rich and famous.
I had a dream that I went to Heaven and came back down.
I had a dream that I was married with kids that will grow up and
                                                          be like me.
I had a dream that I will wake up to the one that I truly love and cherish
                                                          for all my life.
I had a dream that I went to a country where I was loved.
I had a dream that I will buy my mum and auntie the house of
                                                          her dreams.
I had a dream that I was running for President of Jamaica.

Shanique Thomas (15)
Capital City Academy, Willesden

I Have A Dream

I have a dream that people
will not pollute the Earth.
I have a dream that people
will not do drugs or anything
that will hurt their bodies.
I have a dream that people
will not hurt or kill other people
because they feel like it or just for fun
I have a dream that you will dream
these same things, just like I do
so don't be afraid to dream.

Ester Oliveira (13)
Capital City Academy, Willesden

I Have A Dream

I have a dream that one day I will not stay silent,
I have a dream that some day I will see why the world is so violent,
I have this dream.

I have a dream that one day there will be peace,
I have a dream that some day I'll know how it feels,
I have this dream.

I have a dream that one day we will all become one,
I have a dream that some day together we will face the sun,
I have this dream.

Adeeba Chekeri (11)
Capital City Academy, Willesden

World Forgiveness?

A world full of non-inspiration
A lack of enthusiasm to live
Why when we're given this short life
Do people not bother to forgive?

A land with such natural beauty
Destroyed by the wars of this world
Do leaders not think for a minute
That we cannot stop, unite and forgive?

America, China and England,
Three of the world's greatest powers.
With the poverty of such countries as Africa,
Why do they not have money, yet find it so easy to forgive?

Michael Bromfield (14)
Eastwood School, Leigh-on-Sea

I Have A Dream

I have a dream to change poverty and war,
To stop the killing of the poor.
The people of Iraq are dying still,
Many people we shall kill.

I have a dream to stop the stabbing,
The evil people who like child grabbing.
The devil-people who hunt for gore,
Should be locked up for evermore.

The people of Iraq see the fighting,
They feel the desperation and hear the shouting.
The missile explosions are causing death,
People are dying with every breath.

Sam Brown (12)
Eastwood School, Leigh-on-Sea

A Ticking Time Bomb

The innocent are killed without warning,
The explosions echo through the tunnels.
The fear, the panic, the piercing screams,
Terror strikes at any moment.

Destruction and deceit come out to play,
With no warning to grab their prey.
The wrong place at the wrong time,
The blood, the bodies, cold-blooded murder.

The injustice, the cowardice,
Never facing the consequences.
The lies, the hatred, the effects of one's actions.
The silence of death.

Christie Tautz (14)
Eastwood School, Leigh-on-Sea

My Mum

My mum,
My mum was a midwife,
She used to help people at the hospital,
She worked day and night,
Helping people who were pregnant,
Helping mums give birth.
She's kind, caring and thoughtful,
To look after lots of people,
My mum,
My mum worked very hard
To be a midwife
And ever since she was little,
She wanted to be a nurse
And she got the job
And really enjoyed helping people.

My mum,
My mum is the best,
A midwife,
A caring mum
And also a very loving person.
My mum,
My mum,
A midwife,
A caring mum
And also a very loving person.
My mum,
The mother of two children
And cares for others as well
Is the one who inspires me the most!

Gemma Varney (13)
Eastwood School, Leigh-on-Sea

Toil For Oil

Blair and Bush
Stop being cruel,
Treating your people
Like we are fools.

You raid Iraq,
For terrorist groups
And with your greed,
You kill our troops.

You bomb Baghdad
And don't feel bad,
The murdered's family,
Eternally sad.

You invade Basra
And soldiers die,
You say you're upset,
But we know it's a lie.

You start the war,
You want a fight,
But you don't realise,
You're not that bright.

The whole world knows,
You caused this toil,
For one thing only
And that is oil.

Scott MacDonald (15)
Eastwood School, Leigh-on-Sea

I Have A Dream!

I have a dream to see the world
And see the way others live.
I have a dream where people won't need to fight to resolve problems
And then cry in the aftermath.
My dreams are not impossible,
But they feel so far away.

Everyone has a dream,
Whether they are young or old,
Some to be rich and famous,
Some just to have a family.
Every dream is different,
Unique in certain ways,
But every dream has one thing in common,
They are created by looking to the future.

Not everyone will fulfil their dreams,
Though the dreams they may fulfil is that of another person.
Many people are forced to live a life they do not want to lead,
Most by overprotective or out of control parents.
You shouldn't let your dreams be crushed by another being,
You should live your life the way you wish,
Without the interference of others.

My dreams is to see the world
And that's what I'm going to do,
I'm not going to let my dreams be crushed
For the sake of another.
My dream is my dream, no one else's.
Why should I live another person's dream,
Just because they couldn't fulfil it themselves?
Everyone has a dream,
Don't let it be just a dream, live it!

Charlotte Parker (14)
Eastwood School, Leigh-on-Sea

I Have A Dream

I have a dream to help others in need
To soothe their suffering and pain
To heal the hearts that bleed
And to bring out the sun when the skies are blue

I have a dream that cruelty doesn't exist
Where everyone values life
Where a person controls their anger and is able to resist
When no one uses weapons like a knife

I have a dream that abuse will stop
Where a child does not suffer from hunger
Where there is no fear of calling the cops
I don't want this to go on any longer

I have a dream that everyone is equal
Where no one is prejudice
Where we are not called by colour but looked at like ordinary people
Where we respect people's religions and not make them a terrorist

I have a dream that I could be like Martin Luther King
I have a dream that I could help people in need like Bob Geldof
These were ordinary people
Who had the same dream as I
I have a dream to help the world.

Nikita Patel (13)
Eastwood School, Leigh-on-Sea

I Have A Dream

I have a dream
That one day I will change
I will go back to my normal self
I can forget all the bad things that have happened in my past

I have a dream
That I never started the stuff that I do
That makes my life a misery
That brings me down when I should be up

I have a dream
That everyone will accept me soon
That they will not be disgusted in me
I will be accepted back into my family once again

I have a dream
That one day that voice inside my head will leave me
It taunts me in the night
It bullies me and beats me like a vulnerable child

I have a dream
That one day I will not be alone in the dark
That I will be able to be wild and free
That I will have friends that accept me

I have a dream
I will be able to trust in myself again
I will be able to love someone instead of something
I will love someone that would be able to help me

I have a dream
I would be able to fit in somewhere
I won't have people after me
Wanting to get me

I have a dream
That one day I would be me.

Bridie Tarling (14)
Eastwood School, Leigh-on-Sea

I Have A Dream

I have a dream
That the world could be a better place.
I know this will never happen
Because it is in such a state.

I have a dream,
That England won the World Cup.
This will probably happen,
Cos Rooney is first up!

I have a dream,
That Bush would see some sense.
I wish he would make peace
And leave the world to rest.

I have a dream,
That the poor could be rich.
Then nobody would starve to death
And we wouldn't feel so depressed.

I have a dream,
That the world could be a better place.
Then we could all relax
And God could lay to rest.

I have a dream,
That fairy tales would come true.
Then I would find my true love
And be happy all my life through.

Jordan Taylor (15)
Eastwood School, Leigh-on-Sea

I Have A Dream

I have a dream that the death of Jason would never have happened.
He would still be here right now,
I wish that he had never gone on his own,
Wish he was never left alone to walk home.
He was old enough to walk alone,
But he was drunk and stoned - bad habits this kid showed to all
the young ones he knew.
This boy was an impatient, he couldn't wait for his mate,
His head was spinning,
He wanted to get home that's why he left alone.
He stumbled in the road which he would never have known,
The moment I was told was the day I stayed alone,
Wishing I was there to help him get home,
The day came to where he left,
That was the worst day of my life,
I can't explain the way I felt to anyone apart from my mum,
His friends were there which shows they cared,
For one they lost was closest to them,
The days have changed,
Now we know that whatever happens we're never going to be alone,
There's someone special watching us,
That's the boy that we all love.
Wish my dream was to come true.

Carla Childs (15)
Eastwood School, Leigh-on-Sea

I Have A Dream

I have a dream that one day I will be treated the same as everyone else
I have a dream that the whole world will accept me for who I am
I have a dream that I will meet my family I never had or saw
I have a dream that all the pollution in the world would go away

I have a dream that all the poverty in the world would stop
I have a dream that I will help people in their need
I have a dream that I will lead a healthy, normal life
I have a dream that everyone will live in peace and poverty
I have a dream that I will have food, water and clothes

I have a dream that the world is like a blanket that is warm
I have a dream that the world is like a light bulb that switches
                                                    on and off
I have a dream that people will look after what they have got
                                            and not to throw it away
I have a dream that I will be able to meet new people that care
                                                    about me
I have a dream that life will go my way
I have a dream that I will cherish the family I have
I have a dream that I will never let them go, that they live forever

I have a dream that my world is not turned upside down.

Abbey Short (14)
Eastwood School, Leigh-on-Sea

We Have A Dream

We all have a dream
That we can work as a team
To rub out the problems
That we all face

Such as Bush's addiction to war
He just wants more
Getting all his oil
Tearing our lives apart

We have lost our loved ones
To this malicious beast
Let us stop him now
Before we become deceased

Another problem we face is a lack of food
This gets us in the mood
To halt the fattening nations
And spread it all around

Countries like the USA and England are becoming fat
So we should spread our food that
Can help dying people
And make us feel better

As well there is pollution
We all know the solution
Cut out the fossil fuels
And switch to the renewables

That way, we all win
Even the poorest people do
So let's start building
A cleaner, more well-fed, peaceful Earth.

Joshua Ramsey-Blyth (12)
Eastwood School, Leigh-on-Sea

I Have A Dream

I have a dream,
One which allows me to see beyond,
One that lets me look at a perfect future life,
I have a dream,
I saw how a world could be,
One without hatred and greed,
One without poverty and pain,
I have a dream
Of a world where no child suffers,
No hunger is heard
And no tears are shed,
I have a dream,
One where races are equal,
Old are respected
And youths look to their future,
With hopes and joys,
I have a dream,
That people were understanding,
That people could take each other as they come,
I have a dream
That one day,
Our world will be at peace,
Our world will be united,
As one.

Chelsea Mann (15)
Eastwood School, Leigh-on-Sea

If I Could Change One Thing

If I could change one thing,
I'd stop the stabbing of innocent people,
The cold-blooded murder that has no reason,
The evil no one can explain,
The hateful torture caused by someone
Just like the Devil.

So why does this happen?
Is it because people don't think before they act,
Or because they want revenge,
Or for no reason at all?
I guess we will never know,
But the people who cause the pain will.

Every day you hear of a stabbing,
Its not something unsual,
But why isn't it unusual?
It's something we could all do without.

If I could make every knife blunt I would,
If I could lock up every person who has used a knife
To threaten someone I would,
If I could make everyone safe from pain I would.

I have a dream,
That one day stabbing will be stopped
And that people will learn to respect each other
And live in peace.

Megan Parker (13)
Eastwood School, Leigh-on-Sea

I Have A Dream

Terror in the eyes of everything,
Fearful hearts racing,
People running riot,
Souls desperately waiting.

To die or to live?
Is the question in all minds,
No way to get free,
So hope is all they give.

If you could see, how people fear,
The day and night, so clear and real,
Would you wish to hurt
The people, your friends who all live here?

Don't let them be, protect your being,
Prepare yourself for the worst,
Live your life as if it were to end
And never stop yourself from seeing.

The truth is here, here and now,
It's happening everywhere,
All over the world,
To stop it now would be my dream
But all I need to know is how.

I have a dream where people are free,
To come and go with no fear,
To plea no more for freedom or refuge,
To love and cherish their life with glee.

Catherine Clifton (14)
Eastwood School, Leigh-on-Sea

I Have A Dream

I have a dream,
I hope that one day this dream will come true,
The dream that I want,
Is to be a dancer, not just a dancer but a dancer in the West End.

I want to shine,
Like the star I would be,
Just if only I was a dancer,
I would just let it be.

I wish one day that this dream will come
And everything will be as good as,
I want to shine more than anything,
It would be the best thing ever if I got this dream.

I have a dream,
A dream that involved everybody,
I wish that everyone was the same,
By this I mean that people were treated the same,
These days people, who are better at something,
Also get treated better than others.
Everybody is the same as each other, no one is better or worse!
Everybody had some good and bad in them!

Jessica Martin (15)
Eastwood School, Leigh-on-Sea

I Have A Dream

I have a dream that,
In the future,
Things will be alright.

In this dream,
I ruled the world
And stopped all the violence
And crime.

I have a dream,
That premature babies always survived,
So there would be less hate in the world.

I have a dream,
That cancer had a cure,
Not many people would suffer,
Then people would be a lot tougher.

I have a dream that
There would be a light at the end of the tunnel for all
The poor and ill people,
The rich people would give and not just take.

I have a dream
The world would be at peace.

Karyn Clarke (15)
Eastwood School, Leigh-on-Sea

Pointless Boredom

Are you bored?
Why don't you smash up that crummy corner shop?

They don't need their windows,
They don't need their money,
You just think you're hard,
You just think you're funny.

Are you bored again?
Why don't you spray that frugal house?

They don't want it white,
They don't want it clean,
Don't worry about the colours,
Just chuck on a load of green!

Don't tell me you're bored again!
Why don't you swipe something from that shop?

You desperately need it,
It's all by itself,
You can't live without it,
So take it off the shelf!

The shopkeeper stares at a boy
Holding an object, looking forlorn,
He turns to serve a customer
Then turns back and the object is gone.

So why do people do this
When they have no cause at all?
But for them it only hits home,
When it's time for the police to call.

Maybe one day
The odd one out will be
The person who does the stealing
And won't fit in with you and me.

Billie Dolphin (14)
Eastwood School, Leigh-on-Sea

I Have A Dream!

My dream is to become a vet,
My dream is to become a superstar.
My dream is to become a worldwide hairdresser,
My dreams are just that - dreams.
What am I thinking?
Look at me, how could I be so stupid?
Dreams are just a fantasy,
Wonderful and magical but nothing more.

My dream is to become a TV presenter,
My dream is to become a lawyer.
My dream is to become a mum of ten,
But why keep dreaming?
It's not like my dreams are reality,
Life is not a fantasy.
But lives on facts,
That my dreams will just be that!

My dream is to become an astronaut,
My dream is to become a dancer,
My dream is to become a surgeon,
All these dreams can't come true,
Dreams like these don't happen to me,
I'm not getting my hopes up,
Just looking at reality!

Leah Duggan (15)
Eastwood School, Leigh-on-Sea

I Have A Dream . . .

Bombs are flying,
People are dying.
Children are crying
And politicians are lying too.

Chips are frying,
So we are buying
And that's why we're fat,
Enough of that!

Our world is dirty,
Our teens are shirty.
Which adds to war, so much shouting,
So much chaos, evil is sprouting.

This is not my dream,
But a nightmare.
The world must turn to the sun,
To see a bright future.

Danny Bradfield (13)
Eastwood School, Leigh-on-Sea

Bring Us Justice

Your tears that fall
Will not stop this
Your injustice has been done
Your immoral thoughts
Have driven you here
I hope you have great fun.

Two years Sir and no more
Free again to pounce onto the public
To cause never-ending pain and sorrow
'Why no longer?' plea the victims
No one knows
Let the life you have cost the world take yours
I have a dream that someday justice for murderers
And evil-minded people will be done.

Sarah Corroyer (14)
Eastwood School, Leigh-on-Sea

I Have A Dream

Dream of a world without *pollution*.
No devastation,
No smoke,
No weapons of mass destruction.

Dream of a world without *famine*.
No greed,
No desperate people,
No need for extra food.

Dream of a world without *war*.
No drought,
No chaos,
No more people being in desperation.

Think of all of this,
How life would be so much better,
If we could live in a world full of bliss.

Dean Williams (12)
Eastwood School, Leigh-on-Sea

I Have A Dream To Just Be Me

I have a dream to just be me,
Not just one of the crowd.
Copying the media and celebrities,
I want to be unique and proud.

Why should we follow the trend
Where everyone acts as clones?
Individuality should be our strongest end
We are our own blood and bones.

Be true to yourself and in doing so,
The real 'you' will appear.
As a person you will grow,
Just don't turn back in fear.

Misha Alphonse (14)
Eastwood School, Leigh-on-Sea

Dream Of Beauty

What is the beauty of a dream?
The leap into a universe unknown, a wonder
A marvel of images and imagination

Beauty, the sixth wonder
Surely a dream
One that can stop wars and pollution
Stop time

Beauty, a woman that glows as she walks, hair flowing
A cascading waterfall
Where is Earth going to make such destruction?
Alongside the dream of beauty

The one dream that exists, in a world of nightmares
From inner peace
To the outer seduction
A dream
Life
Beauty.

Callum Lagden (15)
Eastwood School, Leigh-on-Sea

I Have A Dream

People only want it for the money
People just don't care about the rest
That's why they want to win the war
So they can be the best.

Guns come out, but people don't care
This war with tanks and guns will kill
People worry about their families
They only want it to stop!

Will it ever stop? Will the gun just drop?
When the people realise that war,
Is a very bad choice?

Tom Bolden (13)
Eastwood School, Leigh-on-Sea

I Have A Dream

I have a dream to work with kids
To get a kick out of it

Have loads of fun
And play cool games
To experiment and have a good day

I think that kids are great
To sit and watch them play
The smiles upon their faces
The bounce in their walk

To help the ones who are in trouble
The ones who are all alone
The ones that don't know what to do
Or the ones that are disowned

So hopefully one day
My dream will come true
I have to study hard
And concentrate on what I like to do!

Hannah Bowell (15)
Eastwood School, Leigh-on-Sea

Pollution

P ollution is destroying the world as we know it,
O il is causing wars as people try to control it,
L osing the battle to stop global warming,
L uring the carbon in the atmosphere to its forming,
U ndecided means of handling this,
T oo many governments giving it a miss,
I neffective means to manage the gases,
O verseas polar ice caps are losing their masses.
N ow we know the effects will show!

Stuart Wright (13)
Eastwood School, Leigh-on-Sea

I Have A Dream

I have a dream, that some day the unforgiving can be forgotten,
that people would be happy and love would be deep,
that there'd be no time to drown your sorrows and weep.
I have a dream, that one day I could see the sky and the birds sing,
the flowers blooming as the day begins.
I have a dream that I couldn't leave you right now because
you are so young, and even though Mummy's going somewhere
special you have to realise that Mummy's not coming home.
I have a dream that this beeping noise would go away and this pain
would no longer be, because all my life I haven't been able to see.
I have a dream that people could look around themselves because
I simply can't and I hope that when people wish for things,
they wish within.
I can't watch my daughter swim, or see her as she grows.
The pain that is in me no one else could know.
To experience the devastation in my heart, I can no longer bare it,
it's too hard.
When I knew it was the last time I would see my precious girl,
I was really weak baby girl, I wanted to sleep.
I remembered the last words I heard you say before I wrote this,
you said, 'Mummy I know you're ill and you want to go now,
but just tell me this; am I pretty?'
I have a dream, that I could have answered you.

Joanna Richards (14)
Eastwood School, Leigh-on-Sea

I Have A Dream!

I hear in the news about the problems in people's lives,
About how some people get stabbed with a knife,
I wish never to be in the news for people to hear about my life,
But will they?

I don't want anyone to come to any harm
And I only want problems that can be sorted by lip balm,
Why do people want to hurt other people?

I wish all my family and friends to be happy and well
And if not I hope they would tell,
If they weren't happy I would be there to help them through
But would they tell?

I wish to be of wealth and have very good health
And I wish I could be proud of myself,
For once in my life,
But will I ever?

I wish to make my parents proud,
So proud they want to shout out loud,
Will that wish ever come true?

I wish everybody to be able to fulfil their dreams,
Without any nasty schemes,
Does everybody have these wishes and dreams too?

Amelia Going (15)
Eastwood School, Leigh-on-Sea

I Have A Dream

I have a dream or so it would seem to help me come through anything

I have a dream to play football with my feet
And to meet players that are top of the heap
For them to teach me all they know,
Fake it and use it so that I will know I will succeed.

I have a dream or so it would seem to help me come through anything

I have a dream there is no poverty
People suffering from the daily racism I don't want any of that
I don't want anything bad happening to good people
It is a selfish act and leaves them feeling alone

I have a dream or so it would seem to help me come through anything

I wish people were not isolated
By people that think they are more important than others
I wish everyone was treated as individuals
Not belittled for being different
Different is good, don't be someone you're not

I wish all these dreams could come true
And the world would be a better place for me and for you.

Rachael Selfe (15)
Eastwood School, Leigh-on-Sea

Graffiti!

G raffiti is everywhere you look,
R ound every corner,
A ll over walls,
F earless hanging from railway halls,
F lats, houses, factories have all been tagged,
I n every single building there is graffiti,
T agging has got out of control, to the artist the world is a wall.
I t is everywhere.

Jamie Hodgson (12)
Eastwood School, Leigh-on-Sea

I See A World . . .

I see a world . . .
Where guns are a regretful invention,
Where war is a distant memory,
Where black and white people live in harmony,
Where stabbings and rape are never experienced,
Where the nearest people get to domestic violence
Is an innocent playfight.

I see a world . . .
Where animals live without fear of humans,
Where trees blow effortlessly in the cool breeze,
Where we love and respect nature,
Where the air is pure and clear,
Where 'endangered species' is no longer a phrase in the dictionary.

I see a world . . .
Where I don't see people's lives crumble,
Where everywhere I look is a smiling face,
Where the ones I love are happy,
Where there's respect for people's feelings,
Where I can bring a smile to someone's face
No matter how much they are crying.

I see a world . . .
Where love is at the top of everyone's list,
Where we look after each other,
Where life is a pleasure not a living hell,
Where everyone has a chance to shine,
But dreams are always better than reality . . .

Amelia Jenner (14)
Eastwood School, Leigh-on-Sea

I Have A Dream

Before computers took over the world
And typewriters were no more.
Before horse and carriage were out of date
And cars were the new-found door.

Money was never a problem,
There were no standards set,
Everyone was an individual
And we all had different respects.

We were never really judged
And we weren't put into groups,
There wasn't a certain style,
Nobody had a class,
We were all just a big collection,
All bunched together as one.

But today we differ
And we depend on everything else.
We have forgotten the way it could have been
And now we have developed too far.

So we need to realise how lucky we are
To live and have others provide for us,
Because other people aren't so fortunate.
Imagine if we had to live like them . . .
What would you do then?

Toni Tomlinson (13)
Eastwood School, Leigh-on-Sea

I Have A Dream

I have a dream,
That racism will stop
And that we all would be *top,*
Honesty would be bold,
No one would fight over gold
And children would do what they're told

I have a dream,
That bullying would halt,
Then to know that it wasn't their fault,
Children will work to the bone,
No more spending hours on the phone.

I have a dream,
That hospitals would be clean
And teachers will not be mean,
I have a dream, that McDonald's will close,
So there will not be any overweight
People on the roads.

I have a dream,
That no one will lose
And so I can buy more shoes
And so can the unfortunate.

I have a dream,
That everyone's life would be lit by a torch
And everyone's hatred would be scorched.

Charlotte Blyth (13)
Eastwood School, Leigh-on-Sea

I Have A Dream

I have a dream that one day
There will be no war but peace
No famine but food
And no poverty
Just countries reunited

I have a dream that one day
No one will argue
Therefore there will be no war
And then no killing

I have a dream that one day
Everyone will have food
Therefore no one will be hungry
And then no famine

I have a dream that one day
No one will be poor
But all people the same
Therefore no poverty

And all countries reunited.

Martin Gordon (13)
Eastwood School, Leigh-on-Sea

Victims

The victims are like shadows
Without any true friends
Loneliness swallows them
Their hearts take long to mend

Taunted day and night
For not being the same
Bullied into dark pits
Never to be seen again

Scared to voice their opinion
In case laughter follows
Worried, scared, in fear
They take a gulp and swallow

Their feelings are broken
Can't express what they think
For fear the bullies will worsen
And make their worlds sink

They wish to live in happiness
Have friends and have fun
They wish to live in peace
To be free like the sun.

Grace Snoxell (14)
Eastwood School, Leigh-on-Sea

I Have A Dream

I have a dream that looks and money
Won't change people's opinions of people
And Dad won't have to pick you up
In a Ferrari to be popular.

I have a dream that I won't see
A defenceless child no more than eight
Holding a rifle with sheer terror in their eyes
Broadcast on the news.

I have a dream that everyone rich or poor
Will be accepted as the beautiful people they are
Not for what they have.

I have a dream the people will grow
To be unique and successful
And their map of life will unfurl
To reveal great challenges ahead.

I have a dream.

Aimée Bose (14)
Eastwood School, Leigh-on-Sea

A Better World

A ll together we can make the world a better place.

B ringing peace to the world would be a great triumph,
E veryone can benefit from it.
T errorism can be no more,
T his I implore.
E veryone can be equal and free,
R espect each other entirely.

W iping out racism can be done,
O vercoming pollution benefits thousands of generations to come,
R un all cars on renewable resources not just some.
L et generations to come inherit a better world,
D on't just dream about it, do it!

Lewis Hobday (13)
Eastwood School, Leigh-on-Sea

I Have A Dream . . .

I have a dream that people will one day be the same,
That no one will be seen as superior
And no one will feel inferior.

When men will not be judged by the colour of their skin
But by their personalities and hearts.

When we will stop being referred to as different societies
And we will just be one.

When children at school will not be tormented
And abused because of their race,
But will be treated equally and fairly.

When murders will not happen simply
Because of the way someone looks
And what's inside will count.

I have a dream when all of these things
Will come true and we will finally live in peace.

Joni Pack-Turner (14)
Eastwood School, Leigh-on-Sea

Child Abuse

I have a dream, that the children were loved,
Kids were not hurt and kids were not shoved.
Where children no longer needed to hide
And they could learn to find and live with pride.

I have a dream that the cruelty will end
And no children would need to pretend.
Where little ones' bones will not be broken,
Words to children were not screamed but spoken.

I have a dream where eyes were not swollen,
No children's lives are ever stolen.
Where children live with no knowledge of fear,
I have a dream; a hope to bring this near.

Charlotte Isaac (14)
Eastwood School, Leigh-on-Sea

I Have A Dream

My dream can come true as,
In my dream I was taken to war,
World War II
I had never seen such a terrible sight before.

All I could hear all around,
Were gunshots and bombs, what a terrible sound.

All I could see was dead bodies on the floor,
Blood everywhere, help! I can't take anymore.
There were trenches dug deep,
Walls built high,
Knocked down buildings,
People started to cry,
Loved ones lost,
Family treasures broken,
A woman wept sorely for her baby girl had been killed,
She sadly got dragged into the battlefield.

Now I know what it's like,
I wish in my dream this would stop,
Peace for the world, no more wars,
As now I know all the damage they cause.

So as you can see my dream can come true,
Anything is achieved as long as you believe,
My dream can come true.

Holly Dormer (12)
Eastwood School, Leigh-on-Sea

Living In Fear

Cruelty, violence and suicides,
Flames, unbelievable noise and death,
Would you wish this upon another
If you had the choice?

Bombs ending with suicide bombers,
Flames ending in tremendous blazes,
Injuries ending with millions of deaths,
Pain, distress and tears.

No reasons or answers,
Unjust happenings and awful circumstances,
A vortex of violent vibes travel through the cities,
Why? Why? Why?

Buses and buildings blown apart,
Victims living in fear of their lives,
Is there such a thing as world peace,
Or is it just a dream?

The tragedy hits and the world explodes,
News travels quicker than many people know,
Everyone has a body clock,
Tick-tock, tick-tock,
In that split second the bomb explodes.

Sarah Porter   (13)
Eastwood School, Leigh-on-Sea

I Have A Dream

I have a dream that abuse will be no more,
That children won't be kicked through the back door,
That children will have an education,
They'd do well in every examination
And they will have a chance in life.

That rich or poor kids won't suffer in pain,
When a murder is announced, influenced by a game,
That rough cities will be closed
And poor kids earn some gold,
That drugs and guns will be gone,
That kids realise they're wrong
And children won't be killed for no reason.

Children in Iraq won't know what is violence,
The jails and gunshots will be nothing but silence,
They'll know what is peace
And they'll be no wars in their streets.
My dream is simple,
That all over the world, they see no mean!

Jessica Osborne (13)
Eastwood School, Leigh-on-Sea

Imagine A World

Imagine a world without war
No more innocent people dying
No more desperation to keep alive
No more orphans whose parents have been killed

Imagine a world without famine
No more children rummaging through dustbins
No more five mile walks for a bucket of water
No more babies screaming for food

Imagine a world without pollution
No more chemicals dumped in rivers
No more grimy air for us to breathe
No more destruction of our planet, Earth.

Jack Jennett (13)
Eastwood School, Leigh-on-Sea

The Animals

Destruction of forests, hurt, pain,
Hunting, extinction, we're under strain.
Suffering, scared, always in fear,
Whenever we see a human come near.

Hunted, caught, trapped, shot,
They'll strip off our fur dead or not.
No compassion, love our value none
Until our bodies are sold and profits have begun.

In zoos and cages, under people's glares,
Faces, pointing, uneasy stares,
Collars, restraints, we are not free,
That is one thing we want to be.

We have a dream that one day,
This cruelty and pain will go away,
That we can live in peace happily
And make this dream a reality.

Demi Lawrence (14)
Eastwood School, Leigh-on-Sea

Vandalism - If We're All

If we're all thinking it, why do we not say our thoughts?
A broken bench and a marked wall,
If we're all seeing it, why do we not look at it?
Another dark streak and another scar,
If we're all wanting it, why do we not try?
When clear streets used to stand tall,
If we're all in it together, why do we not do something?
Rise up and live out those who deface,
If we're all dreaming it, why do we all stand aside?
For the inconsiderate mistake that stains,
If we're all one, our creed is self-explanatory!
If we're all thinking. . . why not say?

Katherine Day (14)
Eastwood School, Leigh-on-Sea

Climate Chaos

I have a dream that people around the world would stop polluting,
They are poisoning the air with carbon dioxide,
Why can't car companies find an alternative fuel instead?
Sometimes I wonder whether people actually know we are killing
the ozone,
We could use bio-ethanol or hydrogen or something else,
just why petrol and diesel,
Animals are choking and dying by the fumes of the factories,
cars and fires,
People just plant more trees and plants to cut down on the
fumes in the air,
They need to walk more and cycle more,
People are cutting down trees to make money,
They could make money in some other way,
and now animals are losing their habitats and it's not helping
the pollution from the cars.
So why are they doing this?
I had a dream and until the countries do something
we are going to get hotter!

James Newman (12)
Eastwood School, Leigh-on-Sea

I Wish

I wish there wasn't any war or disease that kills us all the time,

H ave no worry of death or sickness.
A n Earth kept peaceful without destruction,
V ile black pollution left to us to deal with.
E very death each day leaves us in doubt the next.

A shouting cry of pain in the air leaves us in despair.

D estruction in this chaotic world,
R eaps life from people suffering the pain.
E yes watering with tears when they have died,
A t this time we know we are doomed.
M y only life is to watch this happen and so to wish it never again.

Tristan Sach (12)
Eastwood School, Leigh-on-Sea

They Are But Defenceless Animals

Alone in the darkness of life they cry for help,
Being taunted by strangers they fear for their lives,
Tapping on the cage, odd people peer in,
Drug oppressed they struggle for focus and balance.

Torn from their families and natural environment,
Their dependant lifestyles whither and wilt,
Scared to cry out they become mentally impaired,
Doomed from the beginning, they need a chance of being rescued.

I have a dream, that one day the wild will be respected,
Treated with care and admiration,
Give them hope to begin their forgotten lives again,
How would you feel if you came under such torture?

I have a dream, that we can find ways around this,
They don't deserve to be mistreated and abused,
They are but defenceless animals,
After all, what did they ever do to you?

Rebecca Waghorn (14)
Eastwood School, Leigh-on-Sea

I Have A Dream

I have a dream
A dream to stop death and destruction
And to stop guns and grenades
Going off in Iraq

I have a dream
A dream to stop racism all over the world
And to stop booing at football matches
All over the world

I have a dream
A dream to stop poverty and homelessness
And to stop AIDS and death
In poor countries.

Jamie Faupel (12)
Eastwood School, Leigh-on-Sea

In My Dream

In my dream,
I want to be a footballer.
So I can go over to Africa
And show the people of the world
Poverty.

In my dream,
Poverty will end
And all will be free
Of this evil world.

In my dream,
The world will be liberty
Because this is a world
With hate and war and that should stop.

In my dream,
Famine will perish
And poverty vanish
With the help of several charities
Like Oxfam and The Red Cross.

In my dream,
We will save billions of lives
From death and chaos.

Ben Yates (12)
Eastwood School, Leigh-on-Sea

Rape Reality

I have a dream,
That one day, people could be free,
To roam the streets, day and night,
Without fear of assault!

To feel useless and mistreated,
Defenceless and abused,
Lonely but angry,
How would you feel,

If one day you were all alone
And out of nowhere,
Came a dark figure?
You can't do anything to stop it!

You awaken and realise where you are,
What's happened to you,
Did you just pass out
Or was it something worse?

My dreams can become a reality,
They can also be shattered,
The only way that they can come true,
Is all up to you!

Francesca Kimberley (13)
Eastwood School, Leigh-on-Sea

I Have A Dream

I have a dream,
About the Second World War,
The horrible truth behind the open door,
About the young soldiers that all saw.

The ruffian Germany looking down at others,
The smaller countries uniting as brothers
And the generals acting like their others.

I have a dream,
About the Cold War,
The Russians and the Americans all wanted more,
It goes on but what for?

Threatening to use their nuclear warheads,
While other countries sleep soundly in their beds,
Threatening to press the big button shining red.

I have a dream,
About the Iraqi War,
Getting the oil, more and more,
The soldiers dreading each and every door.

The bombs around them going off,
The civilians hiding in their loft,
In the silence they hear a cough.

I have a dream,
About World War III,
The blood flooding up to the knee,
I hope this will never happen to me.

Soldiers running to their mum
The winning country just having some fun,
I hope this day will never come.

Danny Shilling (14)
Eastwood School, Leigh-on-Sea

I Have A Dream

I have a dream of a world without war
Where peace thrives and people obey the law
I have a dream of a world without pain
No more death, bombs, tanks or planes
I have a dream of a perfect world

I have a dream of a world without decay
Where we finally learn we have to pay
I have a dream of a world without grime
Where the manufacturers of coal, oil and gas stop their crimes
I have a dream of a perfect world

I have a dream of a world without greed
When we realise it's the Third World we need to feed
I have a dream of a world without hunger
Where the old die older and the youths live longer
I have a dream of a perfect world.

Scott Golding (13)
Eastwood School, Leigh-on-Sea

I Have A Dream

I have a dream where the sky is blue
And everything I touch turns brand new.

I have a dream where my room is a cinema
And my breakfast is a giant chocolate bar.

I have a dream where the sea is pink,
And Dr Pepper would be all I drink.

I have a dream where my sister is nice
And everything is a reasonable price.

I have a dream that I'll be famous one day
And the sadness in life would go away.

I have a dream where the sun shines down
And happiness is all around.

Sophie Gander (12)
Eastwood School, Leigh-on-Sea

I Have A Dream

I have a dream,
That the world would be at peace
And will be a better place.

I have a dream,
That racism will stop
And everyone will be equal, as one.

I have a dream,
That bullies won't bully
And victims won't be miserable.

I have a dream,
That there will be no killing
And people will die naturally.

What my dream is about,
I wish there is no meanness around
And everyone will live in peace
Forever and ever, always.

Rachel Cornelius (13)
Eastwood School, Leigh-on-Sea

Free Speech

I have a dream of free speech,
to say what you want,
to let others know your thoughts
and to live your life free of tax,
fear and injustice.
To allow everyone to believe
what they want and to live their lives
best seen fit to them.
To imply your ideas to reality
and to use power for the good
of younger generations.

Danny Cassidy (14)
Eastwood School, Leigh-on-Sea

I Have A Dream

I have a dream at night
When the stars are shining bright
When the world is at rest
My dream is at its best

I'm a fairy in the sky
Bringing peace or so I try
Peace and goodness will be the power
The world as gentle as petals on a flower

I wake up in the night
With my heart beating tight
I shut my eyes and go back to my dream
It's so real so it seems

The people seem so kind
As there is no suffering they will find
Love is so easily spread
Just like butter on a piece of bread

I have my dream every night
But my dreams are never let out of my sight!

Cristina Corallini (12)
Eastwood School, Leigh-on-Sea

I Have A Dream

Pollution is my dream,
It is my dream to stop,
Pollution can kill people even their crops,
We all don't like it but no one cares,
Because everyone causes pollution,
Even with global warming scares

Politicians are doing nothing,
They're not helping one bit,
We need to help them fast and quick,
We can make it happen,
Just by doing simple things,
Like biking to school each day
And recycling more things,
The world could change in a matter of days,
If everyone on the planet managed to change their ways.

James Eaton (12)
Eastwood School, Leigh-on-Sea

I Have A Dream

I have a dream,
That there will be world peace,
War and fighting will be deceased
Yes, I have a dream,
That poverty will end,
Broken hearts will mend,
Yes, yes I have a dream,
That we will all join together
And happiness will be forever.

I wish my dream could last and last,
Never ever, ever pass
But my dream faded away
Maybe some day it will stay.

Rebecca Whiddett (12)
Eastwood School, Leigh-on-Sea

I Have A Dream - Poverty

I have a dream that children stop dying,
And their grieving families stop crying,
Send Africa some scrumptious food,
With all their festivals get them in the mood,
Make their tummies stop rumbling,
And all their voices stop mumbling,
Because they're always sad,
Make them really happy,
So they don't get mad,
And they stop wearing nappies!
They never eat,
When do they get treats?
They always sleep
In the sand, deep, deep, deep!

Help them!

Shannon Hayes (13) & Jordan Hayes
Eastwood School, Leigh-on-Sea

I Have A Dream - Nutty Professor

I have a dream
To be a mad scientist, I'll create a formula to make mud gleam.
I'll make equations,
I'll solve situations
And answer all questions.
I'll blow up test tubes
And do many a great thing
Like making a never-ending ball of string.
By the time I do all this
I'll have no money, all blown on science.
I'll be a tramp sitting by the road . . .

But that won't stop me cracking The Da Vinci Code.

Tom Payne (12)
Eastwood School, Leigh-on-Sea

I Had A Dream

I had a dream to be seen as the best beautician
Do everyone's nails and make them proud
That is my ambition

I had a dream to be a famous dancer
Jazz, modern, tap, ballet
Dance around the top singers
That is the dream I want to be seen

I had a dream to be seen as a singer
Go on 'Top of the Pops'
Sing my song out loud
But this is the dream I want to be seen

But this wasn't what my dream was like
My dream was so horrible
I never knew how lucky I was
To have a mum and dad who tucked me in bed
And have a warm roof over my head.

Rachel Ross (12)
Eastwood School, Leigh-on-Sea

I Had A Dream

I had a dream, a dream of being rich
The richest you could ever be
I would have a limo, a jet, anything I want
But would that really make me happy?
I guess I will never know and that I'll have to live with it,
I am just going to be happy, happy with being me

I had a dream about war and peace
There is too much war, more than we need!
Our dreams can come true with the help from me and you
So just believe in your dreams
You never know
They could come true!

Shannon Desmond (11)
Eastwood School, Leigh-on-Sea

War Poem

War . . . why?
Declared by the old
Yet it's the youth that die

For the government's greed
For what they think we need

War . . . what?
Physical violence
Bloodshed and gunshots

Innocent lives put to an end
Of the brave soldiers they choose to send

War . . . who?
Our country's citizens
People like me and you

Willing to fight till the end
Risking our lives in order to defend.

Clark Cole-Wilkin (13)
Eastwood School, Leigh-on-Sea

I Have A Dream

I stare at the screen,
Horror is all I've seen.
People killing,
And people dying,
People hurt and you hear them crying.
Peace is needed in this messed-up place,
Young men crying with tears on their face,
Starting off they're all loud and nice,
Soon they became as timid as mice.
Their nerves rattle with the sound of a bomb,
Where the heck did that come from?
I have a dream,
To end all war,
To reveal the hidden terror from behind closed doors.

Matthew Saunders (14)
Eastwood School, Leigh-on-Sea

I Have A Dream . . . Poverty

Why are we obese,
Bloated, fat and round?

Why are they starving,
Shrivelled, ribbed and flat?

Why do we ignore it,
Pass by, walk past and look the other way?

Why do they suffer,
Starvation, hunger and famine?

Why do we throw it away,
Waste, trash and bin it?

Why don't we donate,
Give, share and help?

Why?

Matthew Eade (12)
Eastwood School, Leigh-on-Sea

I Have A Dream

The other day
I had this dream
Or so it would seem
There was no badness in the world
And there was no sadness.

I had a dream
Or so it would seem
Everyone stopped dying
Which made everyone stop crying.

I had a dream
Or so it would seem
Everyone was always happy and jolly
Singing, dancing and prancing
And that would be my dream.

Talia Hartley (12)
Eastwood School, Leigh-on-Sea

War Will End Soon

I have a dream that will soon appear,
That one day all will be anti-war,
That all the pain and suffering will disappear,
And the world will be at peace once more.

War isn't helpful for anyone,
It is the bringer of murder and death,
The soldiers continuously fire a gun,
This soon leads to their despair.

But fortunately courage runs through their guts,
They will not be scared to die,
Fighting for their country more than makes up,
For the time they've lost their lives.

Explosions blow privates sky high
And smokescreens fill the field,
Bloodstains on the ground like a redcurrant pie
And bullets lie like a mass of pills.

A small fraction of soldiers survive the war
And we don't want to lose any more,
It will all be over soon enough
And no one else will lose their blood.

Joshua Binder (13)
Eastwood School, Leigh-on-Sea

One Day

One day
There will be trees
Enrobing the Earth
And under the sea

One day
There will be peace
Around the world
The pain will cease

One day
It will be clean
A population
Never seen

One day
We will all die
With evil around us
When above us survives

One day
Life will be gone
So the world
Can just live on.

Michael Darrah (13)
Eastwood School, Leigh-on-Sea

Out Of The Water

Out of the water and onto the beach
Bang, bang, bang
Running about now drop to your knees
Bang, bang, bang
The rattle of gunfire hurting your ears
Bang, bang, bang
You are scared stiff and start dropping tears
Bang, bang, bang
Off the beach and onto the hills
Bang, bang, bang
The bunker on top showers bullets so near
Bang, bang, bang
You have no choice you have to run
Bang, bang, bang
But you are shot flat out by the machine gun
Bang, bang, bang
Out of the water to play on the beach
Bang, bang, bang
Feel the sand beneath your feet
Bang, bang, bang
You have no idea of memories here
Bang, bang, bang
The Normandy beaches were once full of fear
Bang, bang, bang
Off the beach and onto the hills
Bang, bang, bang
You climb to the top to meet with your peers
Bang, bang, bang
You have made your choice you are going to play war
Bang, bang, bang
Then your friend shoots you down and you fall to the floor
Bang, bang, bang

I have a dream, no guns or war but we pay our respects
To those men before.

Reece Mound (14)
Eastwood School, Leigh-on-Sea

Girls

Girls
They stab each other in the back
They fight and make up
But they never learn their lesson
No matter how hard they try.
A secret's always spilt
A finger's always pointed
And a side is always taken.

Girls
They betray each other
They judge and they don't care
But they never see the pain they cause
Once the fight's been thrown up high
A gap is always made
A friendship's always broken
And tears are always shed.

Girls
They speak before they think
Throw accusations
But don't care about the truth.
The truth
That's what matters
That's what a friendship is made of.

Friends
Friends are the ones you should be able to trust.
The ones that know you inside out
And the ones that should always watch your back.

But girls aren't like that
We're not like that.

It's time to change
That time is now.

Sara Elansary (14)
Eastwood School, Leigh-on-Sea

If I Had A Dream

If I had a dream,
I would fly over the world,
Touch the sky
And be free.

If I had a dream,
I would be King of England,
Create the biggest army ever
And be *indestructible*.

If I had a dream,
I would win the World Cup for England.
Be remembered
As a legend.

If I had a dream,
I would be the richest man ever,
Buy West Ham
And win them the League.

If I had a dream,
I would think of all that,
But really,
It's only a *dream*.

Jack Doherty (12)
Eastwood School, Leigh-on-Sea

I Have A Dream

I have a dream,
That the world was young.

I have a dream,
The world was free.

I have a dream,
That birds will dance.

I have a dream,
That frogs will laugh.

I have a dream,
That cats will play.

I have a dream,
That butterflies sing.

I have a dream,
That tortoises drink tea.

I have a dream,
I am happy.

I open my eyes to see,
The dream isn't the world,
The dream's within me.

Alexis Harrison (11)
Eastwood School, Leigh-on-Sea

Sarah Is A Skyline Star

I had a dream last night
This was wild and weird,
With lights shining bright
In my mind I imagined being on stage when people cheered

It was real I was going on stage
Butterflies fluttered in my tummy
I felt trapped in a cage
I just wanted my mummy

When the curtain began to rise
I knew I had to be brave
Oh what a lovely surprise
When everyone waved

The music began to play
My feet began to tap
I began to sway
The audience clapped

The music progressed
I was jumping and leaping
Doing my best
My mum started weeping

When I woke up I realised what the dream was about.
I have to believe in myself and follow my heart

To fame.

Zoe Norris (12)
Eastwood School, Leigh-on-Sea

I Have A Dream, Nelson Mandela's Dream!

I want to help everyone,
I want everyone to have some fun,
I don't want blacks to be bullied by whites,
When this happens I have sleepless nights,
Why does it have to be this way?
I want to see the children play.

The freedom pass we were given I burnt in protest,
For this country I love the best,
I don't want to go back to the way we were,
Although those fun days I did prefer.

I want to make a difference to help everyone,
I want to make a difference to bring back the *fun!*

Eloise Shrimplin (11)
Eastwood School, Leigh-on-Sea

My Dream To Be A Famous Footballer

My dream is to be a footballer
Scoring goals for my team *England!*
Playing with other players
I'm a forward player alongside Rooney
Dodging round all the defenders
Left forward twist
My right foot is pulled right and *smack!*
It's a goal, my first goal for England

My dream is to be a footballer
Scoring goals for my team *England!*

Hannah Monnickendam (12)
Eastwood School, Leigh-on-Sea

Dreams Of No War

I have a dream
That there will be no wars
Everybody will gleam
With hope for our world.

There is great affliction during war
People also get tortured
They wish for peace once more
As they cannot take this pain anymore.

There is much desperation
The hatred for the enemy military
There's been so many temptations
But so much bravery.

Lots of sweat, tears and blood
People killed in an explosion
Soldiers sinking in the wet mud
Only wanting to be home watching television.

Always bullets flying through the air
These soldiers have lost their social skills
How can people dare
Soon they will be going everywhere on wheels.

Heads decapitated,
Legs snapped,
Arms broken,
Necks cracked.

This is why I have a dream,
That there will be no wars,
Everybody will gleam,
With hope for our world,
War no more.

Stevie Mayo (14)
Eastwood School, Leigh-on-Sea

I Have A Dream

I have a dream,
The world is a beautiful place.

I have a dream,
The ocean is clear blue.

I have a dream,
The grass is a radiant green.

I have a dream,
There is not a cloud in the sky.

I have a dream,
The birds whistle with joy.

I have a dream,
The sun gleams down.

I have a dream,
Flowers cover the ground.

I have a dream,
Animals roam the world.

I have a dream,
Rainbows shine strong.

I have a dream,
Bees buzz around.

I have a dream,
Rivers glisten bright.

I have a dream,
Magic fills the world.

If only life was a dream.

Lauren Williams (11)
Eastwood School, Leigh-on-Sea

War On Iraq

I have a dream
A fantastic dream
To stop the war on Iraq
To stop people dying

Every night I hear the scream of people in my head
Every second people are dying
From dangerous weapons
Why can't we stop it?

The bombs are exploding
Soon it will be our country
Their country is nearly destroyed
Due to our destruction

Many people are losing their homes
Tears in people's eyes
Why can't we come home?
When will it be over?

Dylan Dench (12)
Eastwood School, Leigh-on-Sea

I Have A Dream

I have a dream
For the world to work as a team,
To stop deforestation,
To help the nation.

The poles are melting
And they are collapsing
No home for the polar bears
And no one cares.

We must stop the eternal war
And be peaceful forever more
So that's my dream
For the world as a team.

Harley Lazell (13)
Eastwood School, Leigh-on-Sea

I Have A Dream

I have a dream,
A day to play professional football
For Chelsea and England
And to watch England win the World Cup
This summer.

I have a dream,
A dream to run for England
In the Olympics and win gold,
Just like Seb Coe and Kelly Holmes.

I have a dream,
Dreams to stop war, murders and racism
And be part of stopping
All these terrible things.

I have lots of dreams
And I hope, one day
They will all come true.

Jack Harland (11)
Eastwood School, Leigh-on-Sea

War - Make It Stop!

War, war everywhere,
they pick up their guns
but just don't care
who they hurt
or the families in despair . . .

I wish one day it would stop,
the guns would cease fire,
the people would flock,
some injured, some dead.
We can't go on like this.

Adam Pryke (13)
Eastwood School, Leigh-on-Sea

I Have A Dream

I have a dream that all wars have ended,
I have a dream that bullying has stopped,
I have a dream, the world is in peace,
I have a dream that this dream will never stop.

I have a dream that all people live happily,
I have a dream that life is full of fun,
I have a dream that everyone is smiling,
I have a dream that this dream will never stop.

I have a dream that racism never existed,
I have a dream that everyone is treated the same,
I have a dream that everyone is happy,
I have a dream that this dream will never stop.

I have a dream that everyone gets along,
I have a dream that no one feels left out,
I have a dream that life is simple,
I have a dream that this dream will never stop.

I have a dream that wishes come true and with every wish is
happiness,
I have a dream that every anger or sadness will just float away,
I have a dream that everyone is taken seriously,
I have a dream that people never judge people by what they look like.
I have a dream that life is easier.

I have a dream that all war has ended,
I have a dream that bullying has stopped,
I have a dream, the world is in peace,
I have a dream that this dream will never stop.

I have a dream that all people lived happily,
I have a dream that life is full of fun,
I have a dream that everyone is smiling,
I have a dream that this dream will never stop.

I have a dream that I can write my entire dream down
but I feel like I will run out of paper.

Sarah Young (14)
Eastwood School, Leigh-on-Sea

I Have A Dream

I have a dream that the days will roll on endlessly
as life passes me by.
Bad memories will disappear and float into the skies.

I have a dream that dark clouds will gather
and a storm will arise,
bad people will stagger and die.
Left will be happiness roaming the skies.

I have a dream, people will believe in dreaming
and be busy in their thoughts,
wearing a smile and dancing for a while,
they will live in happiness and peace.

I have a dream of a world so silent, so fair,
a woman wearing a white silk dress will be my guide,
my guardian angel will always be there.
She will wrap her loving arms around me
and protect me from dangers around,
her loving smile will comfort me
and I'll never be alone while she's around.

But this is just a dream . . . if only reality was a dream.

Tessa Fyson (12)
Eastwood School, Leigh-on-Sea

I Have A Dream

I have a dream people will stop dying.
I have a dream people will stop crying.
So let's make poverty go away
And stop families starving every day.
I hope you agree poverty should be in the past
So the person who's just died should be the last.

Bobby Jacobs (12)
Eastwood School, Leigh-on-Sea

My Dreams

I have a dream for peace on Earth,
No more wars or people getting hurt.
Everybody smiling, happiness all around,
Evil will be banished, crushed into the ground.

I have a dream to be a princess,
The latest fashions and a royal dress.
My name known across the land
Maids and butlers there to give me a hand.

I have a dream to become a vet,
Saving the lives of people's pets.
Cats, dogs, rabbits and mice,
I'm always there to give out advice.

I have a dream to join the police,
Catching criminals, roaming the streets.
Helping people to move on,
From the terrible things that criminals have done.

Holly Willson (12)
Eastwood School, Leigh-on-Sea

I Dream

I dream of someone I can talk to
I dream of a forever-trusting person
I dream of someone who won't care what I say
I dream of a person who will stick by me
No matter what I do
I dream of a person who won't judge me
I dream of a person who is there all the time
I dreamt that this would happen
It did for a while but then that person moved away
That person I dreamt about was my *dad*

I love you.

Lauren Bastow (14)
Eastwood School, Leigh-on-Sea

I Have A Dream

The other night I had a dream
That really made me think,
Wouldn't it be great if every girl
Could come into school wearing pink

Girls would love to come to school
And show off all their clothes,
Pink bobbles and pink long hair
And pink ties I suppose

The school would be pink crazy
And everybody would see,
Just how much pink suited us
And how it looked on me

So just think to yourself
If you ever have a dream
Would your school be completely pink
Or so it would seem.

Sarah Upton (12)
Eastwood School, Leigh-on-Sea

World Poverty

Wherever you turn your head,
People are shivering without a bed.

People are dying without a trace,
We need to help save the human race.

Not enough food for the world.
People are not giving enough.
People of Africa all look rough.

We need to stop stuffing ourselves
And think about the world.

Lee Woodgate & Lee Hughes (13)
Eastwood School, Leigh-on-Sea

I Have A Dream

I have a dream . . .
A dream where racism is gone
A dream where everyone is equal
A dream where drugs are only used for good
A dream where there are no stabbings and shootings
A dream where you feel safe to be alone at night
A dream where you can smile at people and they smile back
A dream where there is no hate
A dream where children are safe
A dream where everyone has a home
A dream where there are no diseases
A dream where parents cannot worry about their children
                                    walking out of the front door
A dream where nobody has to worry about their appearance
A dream where you can look how you like and wear what you like
                                    and no one laughs
A dream where everyone has food and clean water
A dream where everyone can live in harmony together
A dream where people don't ever steal because they have money
A dream where children can look on the Internet because
                                    there is nothing bad there
A dream where no one is in danger
A dream where you can reach out and touch the stars
A dream where there is no violence
A dream where animals are not harmed
A dream where you can be free
A dream where there is no bullying
A dream where there is no abuse
A dream where you can be as thin or fat as you like
A dream where everyone is happy
A dream where the sun shines
I have a dream . . .

Abbey Andresen (14)
Eastwood School, Leigh-on-Sea

I Have A Dream

I have a dream
That broken hearts will stick together
And countries of the world are one forever
The cold hearts of the warlords
Will warm and melt away the anger
Of the world.
I have a dream,
That streams will babble and flow
And the ocean will shine and glow.
I have a dream
Of golden dresses
Beautiful hair
And a thousand kisses.
I have a dream
My dream is far-fetched
But it's only a dream
And when I think of it
It makes me glad.

Hollie Watkins (12)
Eastwood School, Leigh-on-Sea

I Have A Dream

I have a dream that all the world is underwater.
The fish are horrible and sharks are nice,
Everyone has a family pet dice.
Everyone lives on the coral reef,
All the sharks have white pearly teeth.
At night all the seaweed comes alive,
They dance the night away until five.
Starfish are celebrities that dazzle in the light,
They put on great shows with lots of flashing lights.
The Queen lives up at the top of the sea,
She has a precious box but hides away the key.
I have a dream that all the world is underwater.

Lana Wigmore (13)
Eastwood School, Leigh-on-Sea

You And Me!

I lie awake I try and try,
But I just can't seem to shut my eye.
I think real deep about what you say,
I hear your voice and turn away.

I can't understand why I do,
But there is something in my mind that reminds me of you.
I try to think about you and me,
I've never thought about you so deeply.

The way you look, the way you laugh,
Even your favourite hat, gloves and scarf.
You made me smile, you made me cry,
I really miss your big brown eyes.

Please come back, I miss you so,
There's lots and lots I want you to know.
To see your smile once again,
Will really help me to release some pain.

I dream about you night and day,
I never wanted you to go away.
I'll dream about you all the time,
I really wish you still were mine.

For now I have to go and wait for another day,
Because all I really want is for you to say
I had fun seeing you today.
I'm going to close my eyes really tight
I'm just going to say goodnight.

Ashleigh Blake (14)
Eastwood School, Leigh-on-Sea

Me, Myself And I

I dream, dream
Like nothing before
So far away
On an island alone
Yellow, gold sand
Take up from my hand
As it slips through my fingers.
Being alone is such great fun
Away from my brother and sisters.
But just to think,
I do miss them a bit.
Especially my mum and dad.
But maybe it is not such,
A good idea, as I do love them lots.

Zoë Stacey (12)
Eastwood School, Leigh-on-Sea

How Jason Gardener Influenced Me . . .

It's the time that counts
And how hard you push yourself.
You are against other competitors,
You want to win!
The gun goes off;
You are sprinting as fast as you can,
To come first would be great,
Even better to set a world record.
But just being part of this
Atmosphere gives unbelievable pleasure.
As you run, the shouts of the
Crowd are brilliant.
Then you cross that line.

Kathryn Springett (12)
Eastwood School, Leigh-on-Sea

My Dream

Fast, fast
Slow, slow
Either way
Up I go

Freezing, freezing
Cold, cold
I must do this
I have been told

So high up
Yet so far down
My cheeks are so red
I look like a clown

Lots of rocks
Lots of stones
I hope I don't break any bones

I am cold
I am wet
But this task
Has been set

Heavy clothes
Big fat shoes
But what have I
Got to lose?

Anna Livermore (11)
Eastwood School, Leigh-on-Sea

I Have A Dream

Travelling to London to see a show
Really excited to get there and go

Getting ready to sit in our seats
Giggling and laughing, really enjoying my treat

My nan suddenly said,
'Why don't you go,
Start dancing again
And enjoy all those shows?'

Suddenly the curtains opened
We looked inside
To see all the dancers
Getting ready to hide.

Soon they were ready
For the last dance
The big finale
To jump and prance.

I knew from this moment
I had a dream
To be a dancer
On the big screen.

Claudia Keefe Bignell (12)
Eastwood School, Leigh-on-Sea

It Can Happen . . .

Everyone says you can make it,
I hear it every day,
But all I want to do is make it to the top,
Live the dream that every kid like me will dream tonight.

I want to be famous,
But I want to be me,
Be happy,
With no one to look down at me,
You hear all these stories,
But that isn't going to be me.

I want to stay me,
I won't change how I am,
But till that day arrives,
I'll pretend it's real,
But till then I'll live life to the full,
Like a famous person will . . .

Lauren Seymour (12)
Eastwood School, Leigh-on-Sea

I Dream

I dream you are friendly, kind and caring
Sensitive, loyal and understanding.

I dream you are special, accepting and wise
Truthful and helpful with honest blue eyes.

I dream you are confiding, forgiving, cheerful and bright
I don't know you, but not one bit of spite.

I dream you are one of a kind, different from others
Generous, charming, but not one that smothers.

I dream you are optimistic, thoughtful, happy and game.
But not just another . . . in the long chain.

I dream you are appreciative, calm and precious like gold
My dream won't fade or ever grow old!

Lizzie Izod (13)
Eastwood School, Leigh-on-Sea

I Have A Dream

A girl and I are best friends
We've known each other since reception
But since then we went to different schools
She went to Westcliff and I went to Eastwood.

We kept in touch, but not as much
Then our friendship broke apart
This is because we didn't phone each other as much
I was very upset.

I then had a dream that influenced me
That we would make up, and would be best friends
A few weeks later I phone up
We then both said sorry and made up.

That very moment it reminded me
Of a dream that influenced me.

Lucy Verney (12)
Eastwood School, Leigh-on-Sea

I Have A Dream!

I have a dream every night,

H opefully what's to follow in life
A nimals, that's my dream, I would be so
V ery happy if that comes true!
E very animal, I don't mind,

A s long as I can treat them as though they were mine,

D reams, dreams, do they come true? If they are
R ough or if they are ill,
E ach animal wants some care so,
A s I said, I want to be there, so if
M y dream does come true, I will be there to help
             your animal and to advise you!

Louise Higby (14)
Eastwood School, Leigh-on-Sea

Martin's Dream

(Inspired by 'Face' by Benjamin Zephaniah)

I have a dream about how my life should be,
Dreaming that the crash was never there.

The burns were never on my face,
And my love was still there.

I even became a dancer and a DJ too,
And even became the best gymnast for the school.

Why can't my life be right
And how my life should be?

Why can't I still be in the gang
And still be with the love of my dreams?

Why can't I have my good looks back
And be the normal me again?

Why can't this dream come true
And be the true me?

It's unfair being like this,
And no one even cares.

Why can't this dream be true
And show how my life should be?

Amy Musto (13)
Eastwood School, Leigh-on-Sea

I Have A Dream

I want to explore,
I want to see the world,
I'd love to find out what mysteries,
Have never been told.

I want to be a lawyer,
I want to set things right,
I'd love to be a lawyer,
And fight for rights.

I want to design,
I want to make clothes,
I'd love to make a line of clothes,
That everyone would wear.

I want to adopt a baby,
I want a little girl or boy,
I'd love to adopt from Africa,
I want to help a child.

Eloise Vinson (11)
Eastwood School, Leigh-on-Sea

I Have A Dream

I have a dream to save the world
To end world poverty is a dream of mine.
This is a dream that can become
Reality.

I have a dream to be like people such as
Stevie Wonder and Haile Gebrselassie
Who give money to the poor.

I have a dream to be a person
Who makes world peace,
This might happen.

I have a dream to live to see the world
Joined together in harmony
This is my dream.

Rhiannon Buckley (13)
Eastwood School, Leigh-on-Sea

I Have A Dream

I have a dream of being a fantastic dancer,
Being up on stage with my name in lights.
Dancing about to the music makes me feel good.

Dancing makes me feel pretty with beautiful dresses,
The crowd claps and cheers,
It goes all quiet, pitch-black, we all run off.

I need to get changed quickly but it's so easy.
We all wait till the lady calls us to go on stage,
We wait till the curtains open,
We wait till the music beats,
And we go on the stage to dance.

We wait to dance to the rhythm,
We smile at the audience and they smile back at us,
We bow and run off the stage.

We have to wait till the other people finish
Then it's us all again,
We run off stage before the big finale,
Run as fast as we can,
We get back on stage all together
Where the spotlight hits me
And makes me feel like a star.

Leanne Stock-Gibson (12)
Eastwood School, Leigh-on-Sea

I Have A Dream

A ll over the world, people are dying

W orld scientists are discovering what it's doing
O ur world is dying with us
R ound the world, people are dying
L iving for a while, not if there's pollution
D own on Earth pollution is covering mankind

O ur cars are roaring pollution out of exhaust pipes
F ollowing us in a cloud of pollution

P ollution kills people every day
O n Death Road
L ittle do we know pollution kills us and the ozone layer
L iving on Death Road
U nder a cloud of death
T hinking of death when pollution destroys the ozone layer
I n an ozone layer being destroyed
O n the way to death by lung cancer
N ever mistake pollution.

Samuel Saunders (12)
Eastwood School, Leigh-on-Sea

I Have A Dream

There's no hate, everyone is the same
Where friendship isn't a game
Where having an argument is a crying shame
And no one pushes another out of the frame
Where leading the gang isn't fame

Where everyone hates the word hate
And life is great
Where having friends is just fate
Where no one argues about weight
And where friends haven't got an expiry date

I have a dream where all this is true
Where all my mates are in the same crew
Where everyone has a different point of view
And everyone's mind is renewed
If my dream does come true
All I will say is, 'Thank you'.

Millicent Magadzire (14)
Eastwood School, Leigh-on-Sea

My Dream World

I dream of a world of sunny places,
Of lovely people with happy faces.
My ideal world would be really bright,
With longer daytime and little night.

I'd rid my world of all things creepy,
Especially spiders, they make me weepy.
War and hunger just make me sad,
But Sports Relief and Live Aid help make me glad.

My dream garden will be full of flowers,
All shades of pink cascading in showers.
I'd fill my house with chocolate bars,
Ritz crackers and lots of sweetie jars.

I'd share my dream with all my friends,
Now this is where my dream world ends.

Gemma Wahl (12)
Eastwood School, Leigh-on-Sea

Martin's Dream!

(Inspired by 'Face' by Benjamin Zepaniah)

I had a dream I didn't have a crash,
I would have my girlfriend,
And my face would be back.

I had a dream to be a DJ,
With brilliant talent,
I would be the best.

I had a dream I was with the gang of three,
And everyone would be like me,
As who I am,
And I could see Natalie once again.

I had a dream my feelings would be the same,
I would be a dancer,
And everyone would love me.

Katie Holmes (13)
Eastwood School, Leigh-on-Sea

I Have A Dream . . .

I have a dream,
I dream of it every night.
To do what I want to do in life,
And to come true hopefully it just might.

I want to discover the ocean,
To be a marine biologist would be my dream
And to discover new fish and plants,
Ones that have never been seen.

To train dolphins and all sorts of marine animals,
And to swim the ocean depths.
Marine biology would be a dream,
A dream I would never forget.

I know it might sound weird,
Extraordinary some people may say.
But I know if I work hard,
I will be a marine biologist some day.

Eleanor Fryatt (14)
Eastwood School, Leigh-on-Sea

My Dream

I wish I could look after the whole wide world
I wish I could visit every country in the world
I wish I could be everywhere all the time
Oh I wish, I wish, I wish, I wish, I wish, I wish, I wish

I wish I had lots and lots of money, really rich
I wish I lived in a really huge house or a villa
I wish I lived somewhere really sunny and hot
Oh I wish, I wish, I wish, I wish, I wish, I wish, I wish

I wish I were a famous actress who was always on TV
I wish I was really confident and full of delight
I wish I had lots and lots of really nice clothes
Oh I wish, I wish, I wish, I wish, I wish, I wish, I wish

I wish I were a fantastic dancer
I wish I had the best voice and sang on the TV
Oh I wish, I wish, I wish, I wish, I wish, I wish, I wish
But after all I would rather be me and I'm glad that I am me!

Lucy Martin (13)
Eastwood School, Leigh-on-Sea

I Have A Dream

I have a dream, I have a dream
That everyone can believe in themselves

I have a dream, I have a dream
That we will have faith instead of doing what is wrong

I have a dream, I have a dream
That each and every person can be successful
No matter what will come their way

I have a dream, I have a dream
That people will find cures to keep the world healthy

I have a dream, I have a dream,
That people will become wealthy and live their lives

I have a dream, I have a dream
That you will be yourself and not what people want you to be

I have a dream, I have a dream,
That these dreams will come true.

Amy Langley (13)
Eastwood School, Leigh-on-Sea

The New World And The Old! (I Have A Dream)

I wish one day racism will end.
I wish one day terrorism will just stop.
I wish one day Heaven will send . . .

A world without violence and terror.
A world with justice and peace.
Not a world with discrimination and disease.

Bombing, bombing, bombing, war, war, war,
That is all it is,
Why don't we have peace, happiness and life?
We should live life to the full.

A world without broken families or broken homes,
Not a world with despair and moans.
Be happy, not sad, enjoy life with fun.
Don't have life short and let it be done.

This is the way to live and be happy.
Have peace, not sadness, get on with life.
Just be ready to take it on the chin.
Let it over your head and wait for the next little thing.

Reece Ellis (13)
Eastwood School, Leigh-on-Sea

I Have A Dream

I have a dream, I have a dream, that one day the world will be a happier place.

I have a dream, I have a dream, that each person will have a smile on their face.

I have a dream, a very big dream, that one day a person will eventually say, 'Be yourself, don't care what people think, you're individual and we love you for who you are, not what you want to be!'

I have a dream, I have a dream, that you never change and fade away. I can't stand it when you leave my front door. I ask myself if I'll see you once more.

The last time I saw you, you kissed me and said, 'I'll never forget you. You won't leave me head!'

I love you Nanny, I've done this for you. I knew this was what you wanted me to do!

Just one more kiss from your lips, reaching your forehead would be bliss.

I have a dream, I have a dream, for these dreams to come true. I'll see you up there, I promise you!

Nicola Dimbleby (14)
Eastwood School, Leigh-on-Sea

I Have A Dream

I have a dream,
To be in a football team,
To be a star,
To have a nice car.

I have a dream,
I am so keen,
To play with David James,
I love to play the football games.

I have a dream,
You don't have to be mean,
I'll play for Liverpool,
It'll be so cool.

I have a dream,
To be in a football team,
I'll play for England like Joe Cole,
For England, I'll score a goal.

I have a dream,
To be in a football team,
I won't keep it as if it were mine,
I'll pass from the halfway line.

I have a dream,
To be in a football team,
To be a star,
To have a nice car.

James Casbolt (13)
Eastwood School, Leigh-on-Sea

I Have A Dream

My dream is to end racism!

I have a dream
To end racism,
I hate to starve,
I hate people who talk about me,
I don't like to be abused,
I don't like racism,
I don't like thieves,
I don't like bullies.

Black and whites together,
We will rule the world,
Black and whites not apart,
It will be much easier,
The world will be together,
Just like when created,
And everyone will be nice,
And everyone will be friendly again.

I hate people who take the mickey,
So, everyone, let's stop this now,
So people will stop dying,
Let's stop hunger,
Let's put a stop to it now . . . *stop now!*

Steven Marr (13)
Eastwood School, Leigh-on-Sea

My Dream

My dream is to end world hunger.
Also to end racism.
I would hate to starve.
I would hate to get abused.

People judge race by the face.
The whole of Africa starves.
People start to die of hunger.
Black and white are divided, it makes life hard.
Black and white together makes life easier.

Let's stop this now,
Before more people die of abuse and hunger.
Let's put a full stop to it now!

Let's stop the rate of our fate,
Before love turns into hate.
Injustice, tyranny, oppression and terrorism,
Also have become the order of the day.
Let's stop it now, before more people die.

Aqeel Rafiq (13)
Eastwood School, Leigh-on-Sea

I Have A Dream

I have a dream, I'll be the Queen
And wear the crown jewels
I have a dream, I'll be the Queen
And I'll make up the rules

I have a dream, I'll be the Queen
With a handsome king and a golden ring
I have a dream, I'll be the Queen
A powerful woman who can sing

I have a dream, I'll be the Queen
A zillioniare is what I'll be
I have a dream, I'll be the Queen
And everyone will want to be me

I have a dream, I'll be the Queen
And I will rule the Earth
I have a dream, I'll be the Queen
A life of misery from your birth

I have a dream, I'll be the Queen
Evil, cruel, nasty and mean!

Grace Claxton (11)
Eastwood School, Leigh-on-Sea

Chess

I have a dream to win this
I want to win this fight
I may only be on a chessboard
But as a pawn I have rights

I have a dream to beat them
I want their king to yield
We show no emotion
On the checkered field

I have a dream to take him
I want the whites to break
I want to take a bishop
This is chess for heaven's sake!

I have a dream to win this
Our side is so great
We will corner their leader
And then we'll have checkmate

After the win I feel so great
We blacks are the best
We will fight again very soon
In another game of chess.

Connor Iontton (14)
Eastwood School, Leigh-on-Sea

I Have A Dream

F amilies starve
A merica gets fat
M orbidly obese that's what America is
I ndulge, that's what America does too much
N ever eating, that's what famine is
E nergy with famine, you don't get.

W hat is the point?
A lways at it, no rest
R IP for the soldiers who died

P ointless, that's what it is
O il is over-used
L ittle is done about it
L ure away from fossil fuels
U nderstand the importance of fuel
T ime is running out
I ce caps are melting
O zone layer, that's what's broken down
N o! That's what we should say.

Luke Brown (13)
Eastwood School, Leigh-on-Sea

I Have A Dream!
(Helping animals)

The days can be long and hard for creatures on Earth,
With some eating each other sometimes from birth,
Why do so many not see the thousands of plant foods that abound,
That lie in the waters, air and ground?
Yet some choose the savage ways, even when shown,
That plant foods are best in their abundance grown,
Nature holding us in her arms with peace in mind,
And we act with ignorance, being so blind,
When given to us, our fellow creatures to behold,
We mistreat them in their billions, a story is told,
The horror, the vileness of animal parts being used,
For washing, clothing, sport, experiments and food,
Awake! Those that do not already see,
That animals are as much a part of us as you are to me,
And turn from that which brings wars, famine and disdain,
And listen to the vegans who tell you again
That a real happiness should manifest from birth,
In every soul that comes through Earth,
It's been written from days of old,
So let the civilised evolution begin to unfold,
And grab your heart with joy that would be believed,
None will be sad, harmed or grieved,
It's not a wayward distant dream,
It's a reality check from a heavenly realm!
A dream is a vision and God gave it to me,
One day all men will walk proud and free,
I have a dream to go sailing through the seas,
I have a dream to cure all disease,
I have a dream to stop lives being sold.

Ericha Stephanie Antonio (13)
Eastwood School, Leigh-on-Sea

The Future Begins With You And Me

I have a dream,
To see the world,
But all I can see,
Is a land of pain and people lying to me.

The Earth is poisoned by greed and lies,
From space Earth is an apple,
Rotting from the inside.
The Earth so awful but we deny,
'Cause men keep on killing,
Women sell themselves.
Oh how I dream of a world
Of peace, love and honesty.

When you see a child,
Look into the future, see how they smile,
If we stop this disease plaguing the Earth,
Spreading through us,
We will die and leave behind,
A land of great relief.
So let's all pull together,
And heal the Earth of greed,
Don't wait for someone else to,
Because the future begins with you and me.

Matthew Arrowsmith (14)
Eastwood School, Leigh-on-Sea

Pollution, Pollution

Pollution, pollution,
There's oil in the sea,
People take no action,
It's just left all dirty.

Fishes are dying,
The numbers are going down.
Whales are suffering,
People start to frown.

There are oil spills,
And petrol fumes,
They both will pollute.

Pollution, pollution,
There's oil in the sea,
People take no action,
It's just left all dirty.

Marcus Wan (12)
Eastwood School, Leigh-on-Sea

I Have A Dream

I have a dream
That peace and love will fill the air,
And that everyone will watch and stare,
At the world of laughter and love.
I have a dream
That roses will rise another time
For beauty and grace.
Poverty and misery to end, and in its place
Beauty and peace will form again,
For better or worse and in sickness and in health,
The world as we know it will burn in Hell
And come back to peace and love.
Maybe it will happen, maybe it won't,
But it doesn't stop you from dreaming for the world.

Amy Owen (13)
Eastwood School, Leigh-on-Sea

I Have A Dream . . .

I have a dream,
For the world to be,
A better place
For others to see.

No more hunger,
No more war,
No more suffering,
Let's help the poor.

Everyone equal,
Like it should be,
Let everyone know,
How it feels to be free.

Make me happy,
Let them smile,
Give them love,
Make them feel worthwhile.

I have a dream,
For the world to be,
A better place,
For others to see . . .

Lauren Davies (13)
Eastwood School, Leigh-on-Sea

I Have A Dream

I have a dream
The world would be more fair
People not upset,
No worries or care.

I have a dream
That people would not fight
Peace all round
Day and night.

I have a dream
That there would be no wars
No arguing or shouting
No slamming doors

I have a dream
There would be no deaths
No murders about
No worries left

I have a dream
There would be no guns
Everyone would get along
And all have fun.

Dami Oloyede (13)
Eastwood School, Leigh-on-Sea

My Dream Of Tomorrow

I have a dream of tomorrow,
Where the future is bright and clear,
I have a dream,
Where peace is here.

I have a dream of tomorrow,
Where recycling is green,
I have a dream,
Our world is clean.

I have a dream of tomorrow,
Where rubbish goes in the bin,
I have a dream,
Littering is a sin.

I have a dream of tomorrow,
Where birds sing and flowers grow,
I have a dream,
Where rivers flow.

I have a dream of tomorrow,
Everyone has a smile on their face,
I have a dream,
Our world's a happy place.

Abby Brealey (13)
Eastwood School, Leigh-on-Sea

Martin's Dream!

(Inspired by 'Face' by Benjamin Zepaniah)

I have a dream that this is a dream.
My life is still the same.
When I look back I see the sight
Of when my life had stopped.

I have a dream that this is a dream
Natalie still loves me
When she says, 'I don't want you'
It makes me feel like such a fool.

I have a dream that this is a dream
That the gang of four was true
But when I see the truth within
I know it just can't be.

I have a dream that this is a dream
My love for sport can grow
Gymnastics and in dancing
Just for me to show.

I have a dream that this is a dream
Most of all to be
A normal boy like I was before
A face that I can show.

I have a dream that this is a dream
My life could turn around
But even though I wish and dream
I know it can't be true.

Amy Boswell (14)
Eastwood School, Leigh-on-Sea

I Have A Dream - I Wish The World . . .

I wish the world,
Was always clear,
No one was bad,
There were no tears.
The sky was always filled with blue,
If you were upset,
People would know what to do.
There were no more wars, peace all the time,
No one would feel down, we'd all be fine.

I wish everyone's dream could come true,
Everyone was equal, like me and you,
Babies grew up to be themselves,
Go to Heaven,
Not to Hell.
I had a dream I could fly like a dove,
And that this world could be filled with love.
I wish everything we buy, could be free.
Will this dream come true?
We'll wait and see . . .

Lauren Everett (13)
Eastwood School, Leigh-on-Sea

I Have A Dream

I have a dream
Where the flowers grow,
And wars will never be seen,
For this, the world will never know.

I have a dream,
With no more hate,
With no more suffering,
With everyone as a mate.

I have a dream,
Where there is no rubbish on the floor,
And everyone uses a bin,
No pollution evermore.

I have a dream of tomorrow,
Where the future is bright and clear.

Katie Ellingworth (13)
Eastwood School, Leigh-on-Sea

A Better World

I have a dream that racism's gone
And so has cruelty and abuse.
Guns do not have to be in use
For us to all move on.

Riches have been spread around
So no one will be poor.
Everyone will buy something from the store
And love will go around.

Hunger will completely disappear
Food will be everywhere.
There will be enough to share
And now, you see, the world is clear.

I have a dream of a better world.

Celine James (12)
Lycée Francais Charles de Gaulle, London

I Have A Dream

I have a dream
That one day humans will stop polluting,
And that they will start recycling.

I have a dream
That one day associations will have enough money,
To build a new Africa and a new Asia
An Africa and an Asia where families will have enough food,
And children can go to school and learn how to have jobs
around the world.

I have a dream
That one day beggars on the streets will stand up
And find jobs where they will have enough money to build a family
And live like everybody else.

Those are my dreams
And I hope that one day they will become
True!

Omar Zaghouani (12)
Lycée Francais Charles de Gaulle, London

I Have A Dream

I have a dream about world peace
and everybody being equal.

I have a dream about rich people
giving up a part of their earnings to the poor
so that they don't have to sleep and live
on the streets, begging for money.

I have a dream about humans
looking after the environment
by not using too much petrol
and causing pollution.

I have a dream about cars
being powered-up by electricity
not petrol or diesel.

Christian Kendrick-Brajou (11)
Lycée Francais Charles de Gaulle, London

A Perfect Dream

As I look out of the window
And look at the world around me
I see the world so perfect
Its beauty doesn't cease to blind me

But in its wonderful perfection
There's a problem, what a shame
It's called the human menace
We're killing our world, we're to blame

I had a dream one night
As I was snuggling in bed
I had my little vision
As I lay down my head

It was about the world
Without pain, without denial
With peace and love and after this
You won't feel so suicidal

It's a dream with no poor people
And no obese people eating too much
It's a perfect dream when it comes
To harmony as such.

It's a perfect dream.

Henry Blake (11)
Lycée Francais Charles de Gaulle, London

I Have A Dream

I have a dream
that children should
not suffer in silence.

I have a dream
that children should
be protected from
their abusers.

I have a dream
that children should
have a place to go
if they want to escape
from the abuse.

I have a dream
that they should
be protected from
the bad people
in the world.

I have a dream
that we should
help them and
try and stop
child abusers.

Benjamin Gowie (13)
Lycée Francais Charles de Gaulle, London

I Had A Dream

I had a dream of a world . . .
So perfect that it would sadly be impossible to create
Even God, Himself, could not create this world . . .

This world was only good
There was love and joy only
Everybody was always happy
And nobody could stop their joy.

No evil in this world, not even a bit
No hate or death
Nobody was led into temptation, no jealousy, no hate, no sadness
Hate did not exist, not even in the smallest form imaginable

Everybody accepted their differences
But this wonderful world may only be imagined
As sadly the world is full of hate and anti-socialism
And this imagined world will never exist . . .

Edward Noakes (12)
Lycée Francais Charles de Gaulle, London

I Have A Dream

I have a dream of a world
Where the climate is cooler
And where animals and vegetation are more numbered.
I have a dream of a world
Where no one is poor
Food we will have in plenty
And houses for everyone.
I have a dream of a world
Where everybody will understand each other
Words will come before fists
And where wars will be a legend.

Claire Bate Roullin (12)
Lycée Francais Charles de Gaulle, London

I Have A Dream

The wish of life is upon my heart,
My soul lets out the freedom,
The children of the world stare at the sky,
Full of stars with no reason,

Hope is needed for all the people,
As they're chased out of their country,
Homes and family disappear,
Because everyone's an enemy,

Oh! Love and hate is in the air,
At day and night they stare,
Thinking what has happened here and there,
As they cry out in despair,

Nature stays unhappy,
As the world is collapsing apart,
Because of pollution, war and no solution,
Planet Earth is dark,

To change the world,
That I had seen,
To wish for luck,
I had a dream.

Alexander Blakoe (11)
Lycée Francais Charles de Gaulle, London

My Dream

If there was only a world without war,
I have a hope of an alliance with beings of energy,
I have a wish of allied beings from another world,
I have a dream of a world of nature.

I have a mind of shamans and magicians,
And of a world without poverty,
But what of poverty and abuse?
I own a hope, that none of these existed.

I have a dream of this world.

Thierry Serafin Nadeau (11)
Lycée Francais Charles de Gaulle, London

A Dream

My dream is a world with no pollution
A world with friendly evolution
A land with no rich and no poor
A place with no war
A zone where everybody respects the mighty law
Would be so cool, I bet you so.

An area where everybody is free
To choose whom they want to be
A world with people that don't judge you by your face
Or your race
But your heart
Because you are part
Of the world.

A land with no fears
And no tears
No guns
But only fun.

Yannick Moxon (12)
Lycée Francais Charles de Gaulle, London

I Have A Dream

I have a dream of a world,
A world full of wonders.

Everyone will speak the same language,
And everyone will be equal.
There will be no war,
And the peace will have no end.

There will be no racism,
And the children will never be alone.

I hope that my dream will come true!

Maud de Rohan Willner (12)
Lycée Francais Charles de Gaulle, London

I Have A Dream

I have a dream
A dream to change this scattered world
Men are destroying their own habitat
My dream, to make the world a better place

Their own atmosphere
Destroyed by the bitterness of pollution
How stupid men are
They do not think before they act

Still, there is racism
People kill just because of their colour
Skin is brutalised, mutilated
Because of this bad, sinful world

Why is this world so bad?
What went wrong?
I have a dream
To make the world a better place.

Francis Jackson (13)
Lycée Francais Charles de Gaulle, London

I Have A Dream

My dream is to help poor people
Help them with food,
Help them with water,
Help them with all the things that matter
Social life, school, education, medicine . . .
We should all have the same rights, money . . .
We should be equal.
Each of us should have the chance of going to school,
Eating properly, drinking good water.
For once, we should all see what it's like to be poor
So then we could really understand poverty.

I have a dream
My dream is to be happy!

Alexandra Lochead (12)
Lycée Francais Charles de Gaulle, London

I Have A Dream

I have dreams
Different dreams
Of new countries
Or new species

I have ideas
Crazy ideas
Of different cultures
Respectful cultures

I have goals
The same goals
To make our planet a home
A comfy place

I have illusions
Loads of them
I see a Heaven
Of sharing and kindness

I have visions
20 of them
About all the same
A world without war

I have wishes
Every one of them
Will (hopefully)
Help fight poverty

I have thoughts
Similar thoughts
Of a peaceful world
Of a quiet world

I have desires
Strange desires
That racism will vanish
Hunger will be history

I have nightmares
So many of them
But if my dreams, wishes, thoughts
Come true, then maybe
The world will be perfect.

Marie-Armance Renaud (12)
Lycée Francais Charles de Gaulle, London

I Have A Dream

I have a dream of a perfect existence
Without the need of any resistance
With so many wars raging on
We need more than a fund-raising song
To halt all of man's disasters
That will only pay for sticking plasters
Which for the victims is not enough
Whose lives of anguish are still tough

I have a dream that all this will cease

The world should be a place of liberty
Instead we have despair and poverty
We should not be judged by colour or belief
For we are all the same underneath
I dearly hope we find a solution
To the frightening shadows of pollution
Our only world, our only dream
Let us not make Gaia scream

I have a dream of a life of peace.

Jack George (11)
Lycée Francais Charles de Gaulle, London

I Have A Dream

To dream is a dangerous thing,
It can cause great frustration,
For I dream of liberation.

I dream to be free, to do as I please,
To live in a world, where no one gets teased.

I dream of a day, to run into fields,
Where everyone in the world has sufficient meals.

I dream for all money to be shared,
And to live in a world that really cares.

I dream to start a revolution,
And to make an end to all pollution.

I dream for the world to be a better place,
And to have great respect for every race.

You see my friend, what I say is true,
To dream is a dangerous thing to do.

Kinvara Jenkins (14)
Lycée Francais Charles de Gaulle, London

I Have A Dream

I have a dream
Of a perfect world.
I have a thought
Of a land knowing only peace.
I have an idea
Of a just country.
I have a wonder
Of a great civilisation.
I have a wish
Of a better life.
I have the intention
Of changing the world.
I have a hope
that one day the world will change.

Marie de Noblet (12)
Lycée Francais Charles de Gaulle, London

I Have A Dream

My dream is to have peace
My dream is to have love
My dream is to help children grow up

Teach them how to read
Teach them how to write
Give them food to eat
And give them *love*

My dream is to go around the world
And rescue the animals
Give them names
And give them *love*

My dream is to help nature
To stop people cutting trees
To stop people building houses
On a place where there once were flowers

I have a dream
And that dream
Is to give *love*.

Natacha Zouein (12)
Lycée Francais Charles de Gaulle, London

I Have A Dream

I have a dream,
A dream to change the world,
A dream to change people's lives.

A dream to make the world a better place,
And to make all the changes possible on Earth,
To make it as good as it can be.

My dream is to make people happier,
For all children to have fun,
And for all the adults to have some peace and quiet,
Without the screaming and shouting of the children.

Benjamin Sagnier (12)
Lycée Francais Charles de Gaulle, London

I Have A Dream

I have a dream
That the world will change
That misery will fly away
Hunger will be no longer possible
Just like homeless people lying on the streets

Racism shouldn't exist
Just like child abuse and violence
Imagine how the world would be
Just a few steps and you'll see
All the changes will appear

The war will end
And misery will go away
Homeless people will have homes
And hungry persons will have food
Just imagine all the changes we'll make.

Alexandra Sentuc (11)
Lycée Francais Charles de Gaulle, London

A Real World

A world where people are treated the same,
Is a fair world where no one is to blame.
A brave man came to say what really is true . . .

All people are equal,
No need to push a different person so that they fall,
We are *all* equal.

This man is a pure genius, I say,
We should all be able to play,
But not only our own colour,
Others, who may come from afar.

This would be a real world,
With people who treat each other equally,
With no one being a bully,
This world would be a real world.

Madeleine Wells (11)
Lycée Francais Charles de Gaulle, London

I Have A Dream Of A World

I have a dream that my children and grandchildren would
live in a world of peace.
A world where war would be rejected
Where every disabled person would be accepted
A world where laws would be followed
And where you would be judged by the character you hold

I have a dream where nature would be respected
A world where the water would be clean and blue
Where the air around would be as fresh as new
A world where trees wouldn't be cut and fall
And where there wouldn't be any pollution at all

I have a dream where conditions would be the best
So good that people would live longer
Where everyone would be together
Scientists would work to make the world better
And work to make the love stronger.

I have a dream

Tanguy Raguenez (11)
Lycée Francais Charles de Gaulle, London

Speech

We must not allow people to waste valuable energy,
Driving 4x4s and using up electricity!
We must encourage organisations such as *Greenpeace,*
And by actions make this waste cease!

I have a wish that we live on a planet as pure as a crystal
Where people don't get bitten and they respect their environment,
A planet where feet are used for walking
And not for using the accelerator pedal of a car.

Us humans must take serious actions,
We have created our own assassins!
The time has come to put an end to this.
We must react if we are willing to save our Earth.

Alex Mosey (13)
Lycée Francais Charles de Gaulle, London

I Have A Dream

Imagine
A world where police deal with more crimes
Imagine
A world where you have one hour of school each day
Imagine
A world where you have the longest legs and can walk into
different countries
Imagine
A world where you don't have to work and money falls from the sky
instead of rain
Imagine
A world where you can change the weather with wishes
Imagine
A world where you can click your fingers to get everything you want
Imagine
A world where you can wash the Earth from all things bad
Imagine
A world where you don't have school bags
Imagine
A world where nothing happens horribly
Imagine
A world where you don't get bad marks
Imagine
A world where you would be magic
Imagine
A world where everything is free
Imagine
A world where only babies exist
Imagine
A world where everything smells nice
Imagine
A world where you never age
Imagine
A world where nobody swears
Imagine
A world where nobody does anything wrong

Imagine
A world where there is no noise whatsoever
Imagine
A world where you can predict what is going to happen in the future
Imagine
A world where the weather is never too cold or too hot
Imagine
A world where you never feel embarrassed
Imagine
A world where nothing gets damaged
Imagine
A world where nothing ever gets lost
Imagine
A world where you never get worried
Imagine
A world where you never get sad
Imagine
A world where you are always happy
Imagine
A world where everything is perfect
Imagine
A world where nobody ever goes missing
Imagine
A world where nothing ever breaks
Imagine
A world where babies are well-behaved
Imagine
A world where you never get injured
Imagine
A world where your country always wins the football World Cup
Imagine
A world where everyone is the same size
Imagine
A world where you never buy horrible food
Imagine
A world where you never buy clothes you don't like
Imagine
A world where books are only nice
Imagine
A world where every lesson at school is interesting

Imagine
A world where you never lose your friends
Imagine
A world where sweets aren't bad for your teeth
Imagine
A world where you never get paper cuts

Think
Would all of this be that nice?

Aurelie Coignard (12)
Lycée Francais Charles de Gaulle, London

I Once Had A Dream

I once had a dream that pimps had become hardworking men
and treated women respectfully.

I once had a dream that prostitutes were self-sufficient women
with an honest husband and job.

I once had a dream that African women would eat at the same
time as men, instead of watching them.

I once had a dream that domestic violence was unknown
to the world and would be forever.

I once had a dream that angels would protect women from men
if the women did not want to be touched.

I once had a dream that divorce did not exist and marriage
would seal love together.

I once had a dream
men respected women.

I once had a dream.

Bakhari Diabate (12)
Lycée Francais Charles de Gaulle, London

I Have A Dream

Peace, liberty, equality. Three of my dreams.
I hope they will come true.

Why these wars, my friends? Why kill ourselves? Why suffer?
We are not cats, we do not have nine lives; we only have one
and we must live it out in peace, not in fear of being killed by a terrorist
bomb! I hope one day everybody will live in harmony.
No wars to fear, no terrorists to hate, no victims to weep.
Just peace.

Everybody, and I mean everybody, should be equal to each other.
Nobody will be tolerated if they enslave somebody or someone
in my country. Neither will they be tolerated if they ill-treat people
in my country. I will try to literally eradicate violence and mugging with
such force that it will change the face of the Earth.
Everybody will be happy. This reality seems far away, but I tell you,
never ever, ever, give up. There is always hope.
This is a dark, corrupt world but, like I say, after the darkness
there is always light.

Yannick Magloire (12)
Lycée Francais Charles de Gaulle, London

Changes

I would deeply desire
That people in this infamous world,
Understand the diversity of races,
Whether it is black or white.

I cannot observe any difference between black and white.
What are the sources of this unjustified discrimination?

Same eyes, same hands, fed by the same means,
Hurt by the same weapons.

Subject to the same diseases,
Healed by the same means
Warmed by the summer.

Maurice Baz (13)
Lycée Francais Charles de Gaulle, London

I Have A Dream

I have a dream where every human being will respect each other, never fight anymore and never judge someone by his physical appearance.

I have a dream where there will be no war, where every country will agree with each other and where nuclear bombs and all guns won't exist anymore.

I have a dream where every human being will accept someone's religion without making any criticism or remarks.

I have a dream where drugs won't be taken anymore and the word 'suffering' will have no meaning . . .

I have a dream where women and men will be equal and where there will be no more sexism.

I have a dream where every poor and rich person will have the same rights.

I have a dream where Africa becomes Europe . . .

I have a dream where no one will kill each other anymore.

I have a dream where everyone will have the same possibility to go to school and learn so as to have a job in the future.

I have a dream where everyone on this planet will respect nature without throwing their rubbish in the sea and the forest . . .

I have a dream where every human being will be friendly with every animal.

I have a dream where every person will be able to eat as much as they like and not starve to death.

I have a dream where every toxic gas that flies in the air will be replaced by something better.

I have a dream where no one will ever be sick again.

I have a dream where no more crimes will ever be committed.

I have a dream where different cultures will celebrate together.

I have a dream of a perfect dream . . .

Laetitia Saad (13)
Lycée Francais Charles de Gaulle, London

I Have A Dream: A World Without Hunger

I have a dream
For a world without hunger,
Is that but a dream?
Everyone eating to their needs.

No more children crying of hunger
The parents watching with despair,
They themselves ravenous
But still not able to feed them.

Is it just that some
Can afford a five-star lunch
And others only the smallest amount of rice?
Is this democratic?

Where do your shoes come from?
China? Cambodia? Vietnam?
People working for minimal wages
Or sometimes children who should be at school.

They might be young
But to keep their families alive,
They work,
Tired and hungry.

Is this right,
That because you are poor,
You are treated inhumanely?
Life goes on for you, but what about them?

I have a dream,
An equal world
No more hunger, no more injustice
I hope it will become more than a dream.

Cordelia Long (12)
Lycée Francais Charles de Gaulle, London

I Have A Dream - A World That Is United

I have a dream,
That poor and rich
Will be united
But not selfish.
All the rich should give money
To people in the streets
And also to charity.

Some people lie in the cold all winter
With only a blanket on,
Filled up with shivers.
They only have a dog
To keep them company,
But the rich have all the jewellery.

Just give a house to the poor,
Not stay at home in your castle,
It is not fair for these people
Who live off bread
And are as thin as a needle.

Be generous to those thousands
Who wait for you in patience and hunger
Life should be a great experience
But not a threat to those people
Who are waiting to be fed.

I dream of a world without greed,
Of a world with equality
And changes we have never seen
All these people who demand a change
Stand up with me
And cry out loud,
'We people, stand in the crowd
Wishing to be helped,
And lie in a warm and hot bed,
We protest against the world
That threatens us
And work every day
We want to be trusted.'

I have a dream,
To help all the poor
Get through their lives without danger.
Help me to make my dream come true.

Celine Mugica (12)
Lycée Francais Charles de Gaulle, London

I Have A Dream

I have a dream
that the world was a different place
that there was no prejudice
and people didn't judge you by the colour of your skin

In my dream
we didn't judge you by your nationality
and there were no wars

I have a dream
that cultures were celebrated and not oppressed
people were open about their beliefs

I have a dream
where certain religions weren't judged
but appreciated and loved

I have a dream
where people didn't hide their beliefs
but showed them and were proud of them.

Dreaming does not mean it will happen.

Amna Radwan (13)
Lycée Francais Charles de Gaulle, London

I Had A Dream

I had a dream of a world very different from the one we live in now,
A world which is fair. Do you dream the same . . . ?

I had a dream of a world which was equal and fair.

H undreds of times I have wished for a peaceful world;
A world where everyone lives in happiness, without fear.
D o some countries have to live in poverty?

A sk yourself, how many children in this world work?

D o they have freedom or a chance to be successful in life?
R eally, is it fair that some live in the worst conditions,
E ven when others live in proper houses with heating and
clean water?

A llowing such things to happen in our world
M akes it an unfair, unmerciful place to live

Ask yourself, is this what you want?

I had a dream of a world very different from the one we live in now,
A world which is fair in all ways. Do you dream the same?

W hy should women get paid less then men,
O r why should women be less important than men?
M aybe this world is simply sexist and unfair towards women.
E verywhere in the world women are mistreated,
N umerous countries don't allow women to live freely

R ighteousness throughout the world would be
I nfinitely good. Is it fair that some
G irls know that when they grow up their
H usbands will have more advantages than them?
T his is discrimination but many think not.
S adly in some countries, this is everyday life.

Ask yourself, is this discrimination or normality?

Alexia McKenney (13)
Lycée Francais Charles de Gaulle, London

I Had A Dream

I had a dream
That the world wasn't so superficial
People were strong and independent
Jealousy and envy didn't exist.

I had a dream
That only inner beauty was valued
Physical aspects were only minor
I had a dream that everyone was loved for who they were
Not who they pretended to be.

In my dream
Stereotypes didn't exist
Everyone was individual
If you didn't think like someone else,
No one judged you for it.

In my dream
Beauty was truly subjective
And perfection was a foreign concept
Groups were formed only by friendship
And popularity had been erased.

In my dream
I wasn't judged on what I wore or I listened to
People looked deeper inside the depths of my soul
And they found the real me.

Sometimes I look in the mirror and think
Who is that girl I see, staring straight back at me,
When will my reflection show who I am inside?

'Why must we all conceal what we think, how we feel?
Must there be a secret me
I'm forced to hide?' . . . Christina Aguilera

'I'd rather be hated for who I am,
Than loved for who I'm not,
The worst crime is faking it.' . . . Kurt Cobain

I had a dream
That the world was a better place . . .

Constance Cerf (13)
Lycée Francais Charles de Gaulle, London

Changing

Once, during a stormy night, while the wind roared,
While the rain poured and poured, never seeming to stop,
Someone came to me as I was sleeping and whispered in my ear,

'Do you hear the blowing of the wind? It is the last breath of
entire populations.
Do you hear the thunder? It is the screams of people
dying everywhere.
Do you see the lightning of prejudice? It is the terrible discrimination,
quicker than anything.
Do you hear the voice of the heavy rain? It is the cries of thousands
begging for food.
Every day means suffering to them, every moment is a nightmare from
which they cannot escape.
Do you feel the night, the stillness? It is the sensation of emptiness,
abandon and loneliness.'

'A small boy is crouched on the ground, tormented by hunger.
He is six and, already, he is alone. People turn deaf, blind and mute
when they pass near him.
It seems like a wall was erected between them. They are so close . . .
and yet so far.
Just like you are such close proximity to a happier world, where love
and peace would mean something, and at the same time, so distant
and different from it.
However, this is your chance of doing the right thing.
You could approach gradually, slowly but surely this better place,
And change little by little the world you live in.'

'This is your world,
These are the people you know, these are the ones you won't
ever meet.
This is the person you will never understand, this is the boy you bullied
and made suffer at school.
This is the girl you might have fallen in love with.
This is the woman you will never see again.
This is the family, these are the children, this is the joy you could
have had, but you turned your back on them.

However this is your chance of doing the right thing,
The opportunity you will not ever get again, this is the chance
you have.
Now is the time to take it and help change the world.'

I believed in that strange visit, in that singular voice.
It is the reason I am here today,
Telling you as that person once said to me:
This is our chance to change and we must take it before it is too late.

Beatrice Di Francesco (13)
Lycée Francais Charles de Gaulle, London

Imagine

Imagine a world where animals have a lot more rights,
Where fish are never detonated from the sea by greedy fishermen,
Where monkeys aren't farmed to be shot at by tourists for fun,
Where elephants aren't snared by poachers to make trinkets
                                            from their tusks,
Or where rhinos aren't murdered for their horns to be ground
                                            into a potion for love.

Imagine a world where loggers aren't allowed to tear jungles down,
Where no industry pollutes the rivers, land or air,
Where builders don't destroy, even a robin's habitat,
Where gardeners don't use poisons to decimate insects and
                                            wild flowers,
Or where people don't leave plastic litter that birds choke on,
                                            mistaking it for food.

Imagine a world where people hug instead of shouting,
Where men talk instead of fighting,
Where people create beauty instead of destroying it,
Where people laugh happily instead of crying,
And where people love instead of hating.

Oh, what a wonderful world that would be!

Persephone Pickering (13)
Lycée Francais Charles de Gaulle, London

Imagine

(Inspired by 'Imagine' by John Lennon)

Imagine that there is no religion,
No people fighting over someone powerful,
No Hell below us,
Above us only sky,
And people living for today.

No people dying over the sake of a cross,
No people getting cursed or blessed,
Everyone being equal,
Living for themselves,
No worries, wills or wishes.

Imagine that there is no class,
It isn't hard if you try,
No good or bad blood,
Just pure fun and happiness,
Living day by day.

No rich and no poor,
The world being a peaceful family,
Standing up for one another,
With the flow of love never-ending,
Never a better day than today.

Imagine a world where birth and death
Are both considered new beginnings,
Where each generation is just as worthy,
Where everybody is happy being who they are,
And no one could think of life a better place.

A world without hate, jealousy and anger,
Where no pain or misfortune is about,
Where colour, class and religion are valued in equal amounts
And extraordinary is a vital remedy.
If my dream of life was to come true, then
People would praise every last moment of life
As much as they would do the first.

Gemma Montalto (13)
Lycée Francais Charles de Gaulle, London

I Have A Dream

I have a dream of a world with no violence
Of a world with no danger
This world is flawless though only a dream
A world that I will hopefully one day like to see
A safer world

Where people aren't scared to leave their homes
Or to go out at night
This world is a better place, a safer place
For our children to grow up in

Another dream of mine, this is all it is
One of the millions I have each day, each month, each year
As everyone has hopes for their dreams to become reality.
However, I am not the only person to have a dream
I care for a safer future.

For my dream to come true, everyone must co-operate
To live in this world would be perfection, only existing in dreams.

Aya Fathallah (13)
Lycée Francais Charles de Gaulle, London

We All Have A Dream

We all have a dream, it is to save our dear planet,
Make Earth a better place for our sons and daughters,
And help humanity live longer . . .

But for that, my friends, we must decrease negative things,
Such as pollution, deforestation, war and more terrible actions
We have created.

We have unleashed these monsters,
So we must be able to destroy them, finish them, cease them!
And we do, my friends, have the power to stop them . . .

We must use all this money we own,
To preserve our green forests that are so important to us,
Care for them, protect them, but not burn them!
Forests like the Amazon provide us with oxygen,
We must use it!

We do, yes we do, have the means to decrease that least
We call pollution: electric cars, bicycles, respectful citizens,
Electricity provided by the wind or the sun . . .

As for the war, it is, my friends, the most insignificant
scourge I have heard of, and I am sure that the majority of present
people will agree with my statement!
We do not even know the reason for these deadly battles.
They cost much, both in money and lives!

Let us put an end to these predators! We must act if we wish
To realise our dream!

Nicolas Voirin (13)
Lycée Francais Charles de Gaulle, London

I Had A Dream

I once imagined the world with no killings, suicide or drugs.
I wish the world could open its eyes and see the love around them.
People are depressed because they're lonely.
People want to commit suicide because they can't find the love
                                                    they want.
I mean, look around you, there is not one day you'd not hear
there has been a murder either in a newspaper or on TV.
(It's mostly apparent accident or crew dealings,
or honour killings for pride,
or wives killing their husbands for treachery or vice versa.
Lots of kids are in orphanages, or in social service care and it's
because the parents gave up on them.
Think about it, this world was not created for all this rubbish,
we have to live in harmony and respect each other.
Family problems occur in all this as well.
So, to summarise, I would like a peaceful world.

Johnson Judichael (12)
Lycée Francais Charles de Gaulle, London

I Have A Dream That . . .

I have a dream that there is no black and white
That everyone deserves to possess the same right.
I have a dream that poverty does not exist
That the world doesn't fear injustice.
I have a dream that everyone will be in love
That everyone is as pure as a white dove.
I have a dream that people will be the heat
That people will be the beat.
I have a dream that everyone is a believer
That the colour of the skin doesn't matter.
I have a dream that nature will be respected
That no pollution will be ejected.
I have a dream
And this dream should be today.

Cyril Giraud (13)
Lycée Francais Charles de Gaulle, London

Change

You see the world in different ways
The same old world on different days
The fights and wars that have begun
The best battles we have won

We want to stop this crazy world
Being twisted round, turned and hurled
Making conflict between our Earth
Killing others for what's not worth

Did you have a dream that this would change?
Did you have a dream that wasn't so strange?
Did you ever cry for our planet's mistake?
Would you ever die for a change you would make?

If you could change your dreams to reality
If you could twist your thoughts to actuality
If you could make a change that you would die for
And try not to remember what went before

Make this dream that you have come true
Make your darkest skies turn to blue
Create something that could change all
It wouldn't make you feel so small

Stand out of the crowd, give your speech
Tell the words that will make you teach
It's time for you to be the best
Now is the time for you to suggest

Did you have a dream, it would be this way?
Do you always wish your dream happened today?
All our lives we've been waiting for this something
Something that would come but could lead to nothing

Endlessly we all wait for a change to come
Not knowing what, one day, we might all become.

Tom Fry (13)
Lycée Francais Charles de Gaulle, London

I Dreamt

I dreamt
There was world peace
I dreamt
Racism didn't exist
I dreamt
School was easier
I dreamt
Cancer didn't exist
I dreamt
Less people would get murdered
I dreamt
It was always summer or winter
I dreamt
People lived longer
I dreamt
The world was a happier place
I dreamt
Smoking didn't harm you
I dreamt
Religion didn't matter
I dreamt
All people were equal.

But after all, it was just a dream!

Liza Anderson
Lycée Francais Charles de Gaulle, London

My Dream

I have a dream,
A dream where there is no war,
No killing, no bombing, no kidnapping, I have a dream.
I have a dream, a dream where every country lives in peace,
A dream where there is no starvation,
Where there is plenty of water.
I have a dream,
A dream where there are no dictators,
A dream where prisons are empty.
There should be no murderers, no pimps, no drug dealers
                                        in this world.
There should be more nurses, doctors, firemen, people that actually
help the world.
I wish racism didn't exist,
I wish the word, 'discrimination' had never appeared.
I have a dream that children will live in peace
And not be sexually abused or raped.
I wish paedophiles didn't exist.
I wish every human being was equal.
I wish women had the same rights as men,
I have a dream . . .
Just a dream!

Henry Awit (12)
Lycée Francais Charles de Gaulle, London

I Have A Dream

I dream about a world, a world far, far away from where I live now.
Without racists walking in the streets,
without teenagers burning, breaking, destroying,
burgling houses and mugging people.

I dream about a world, a world far, far away from where I live now.
With no insects whatsoever, the sun shining like a diamond
and the sea so crystal-clear, like a crystal ball itself.

I dream about a world, a world far, far away from where I live now.
People who are cruel to their cats and dogs,
parents who treat their children really badly,
all of that should just go away.

I dream about a world, a world far, far away from where I live now.
A place where the human race doesn't die
and all illnesses like AIDS and cancer don't exist.

I dream about a world, a world far, far away from where I live now.
Where everyone is happy
and no one is sad.
Although what I'm writing
is not real . . . it's just a dream.

Alexandra Coste (12)
Lycée Francais Charles de Gaulle, London

The Ones Who Are Strong

Every three seconds someone with a dream,
Passes away down life's long stream.
This team we have can break in two,
It's not fun for me, how about you?
When the world breaks up, argues and fights,
It will ruin more than just one or two lives,
But the people who fight to stay hanging on,
They are the ones, the ones who are strong.
The children who can't understand what's right,
The ones who deal with their parents at night.
Those who cry, sleeping out on the street,
Just begging for money for something to eat.
But the ones who block out all bad things going on,
They're not the ones, the ones who are strong.
Those who ignore important situations,
Trying to make up their own constellations,
The ones who need help but deny it in shame,
The ones who cry out for someone to blame.
The ones who sit and weep all day long,
They're not the ones, the ones who are strong -
There are so few warriors, so many tears,
So many people, with too many fears . . .

Isabelle Chevalier (14)
Lycée Francais Charles de Gaulle, London

Imagine A World

I imagine a world of perfection,
A haven, if you like,
Where all around us is so beautiful,
And nothing has a price.
A place where the streets wear happy faces;
Beggars are transparent.
And where your day consists of avoiding
The leaflet-giving man.

I move past thousands of busy people,
Sweat, smoke, cough, pant.
The painted walls of their family homes,
Littered with insect corpses.
I also see the millionaire poor . . .
Always in need of more.

All this life makes me turn my head in shame
Greed, stealth, ignorance, pain.
What is happiness? What is perfection?
Unimaginable.
However much you shock or terrify,
People will never change,
Human nature will always stay the same
Then why do I imagine?

Sarah Burgess (13)
Lycée Francais Charles de Gaulle, London

I Have A Dream

I have a dream where my friend and I will grow up
in a safe and friendly environment.
I have a dream where war is unspoken of everywhere
I have a dream where the world will live in harmony
and not in war.
I have a dream where sorrow is gone and no one is scared,
where no one is ashamed of the colour of their skin.
Where religions are respected, no matter what they are.
I have a dream where heads of state shake hands
and laugh together.
I have a dream where people will not be judged by their
appearance and their religion, but by their character.
I have a dream where black and white people live in peace
and not in conflict.
I have a dream where sexism is no more and men and women
live alike with the same rights.

I want more than anything that peace, equality and liberty
co-exist in this world.

Daniel Sibal (13)
Lycée Francais Charles de Gaulle, London

I Have A Vision

I have a vision that one day all men will be equal,
that nuclear will be history,
that people of all races will be as one,
that, one day, is my vision of peace.

But my main dream and vision is that once again,
grass and vegetation grow on the verdant hills,
that modern constructions are no more
and are replaced by trees.

Soon there will be no flowers and plants.
Us humans are the evildoers here.
If we do not stand up against this pollution,
there will be no joy in our lives.
We must act, for the sake of the world's sanity and peace.

I have a vision that one day, vegetation, plants, flowers,
grass, vines and moss will grow on even the sturdiest
and tallest of towers.

I have a vision that nature will rule once again.

Jules Gibbons (12)
Lycée Francais Charles de Gaulle, London

Worst Case Scenario

Yesterday, yahoos were making fun of a fat kid.
Someone asked, 'Why are you doing that?'
Their leader replied, 'It's fun.
Besides, what's the worst that can happen?'
Tomorrow, the boy will hang himself.

A junkie gave a kid some drugs,
'I won't take it!' he cried
'Come on,' the other replied
'What's the worst that can happen?'
The boy took an overdose and slipped into a coma.

In an alley a group of boys were beating up a kid
'Leave me alone,' he sobbed.
'No!' they shouted and one said,
'What are you gonna do? Cry for your mommy?'
The next day, the kid shot them all with his father's gun.

You may not consider this wrong but sins are always small
And they hurt people.
I know, I have a bullet in my arm to prove it.

Evan Lawson (14)
Lycée Francais Charles de Gaulle, London

Difference

Why are people scared of difference?
Black, white, big or small
What does it matter all in all?
We are all human,
All have hearts, all have brains,
We all have blood running through our veins.
How many crusades do we have to fight
Before we realise it's not right?

I dreamed last night
Everyone was the same,
Nothing seemed right,
Life had no aim.
Same religion, same colour and same race
It was such a dreary place.
Explorers would travel far, far away
Looking for new places day after day,
But all that they would find,
Would be exactly, what they left behind.

Dora Ash Sakula (14)
Lycée Francais Charles de Gaulle, London

Terrors Of Our Land

We always see them in the media
Talking about a better world
About freedom.
They take away our loved ones
Force them to kill our 'enemies' with guns.

Our ancestors taught us if we had to lie
Let it only be used to tell the truth
All we see is men lying to cover up the truth
They're teaching lies to our children
Showing them it's OK to kill
They'll grow up in hate and disappointment.

These men, this government, have brainwashed us
They turned love into hate
They turned pride into shame
They turned reality into cruelty
They turned justice into torture.

They made us hate each other
Different race
Different colour
Just a different base.

All we see in life is propaganda
They fight wars for a piece of ground
So I ask you, for justice, raise your hand
There are some who need us to be grand
Truly, these men, this government, are the true terrors of our land.

Sahar Gadel Kareem (14)
Lycée Francais Charles de Gaulle, London

A Dream Of The Future

The wars were over, the skies were blue
There was love between all who grew.

There was one man who made us change
He was quite small and not great of age.

He had a dream of helping me,
You and they and the ones who weren't free.

He helped a man who passed it on
And it is now something that can't go wrong.

The world had changed
Everyone was strong
They were dancing and singing to the same song.

The colours were not black and grey,
But pure and light to brighten the day.

This pattern was as hard as rock,
It went round like a ticking clock.

Eloise Best (14)
Lycée Francais Charles de Gaulle, London

I Have A Dream

The world we live in is anything but perfect;
violence plays a huge role in why that is so.
There are people living in horrendous conditions with no heating,
no family, no beds . . .
And we are the ones that are letting this slide.
But all this can be stopped:
unwanted clothes can be donated and money can kindly
be given to charities.
Everyone who can, should try to help in any way they can.
Drugs, racism and vandalism can disappear with just a little
persistence from all of you.
I wonder what a stranger would say coming into this world?
Or how a baby would first react at birth if given the early gift
of speech?
Are you impressed with what you see in this world?
Are you proud of all the crime that is going on at this present moment?
Obviously you, yourself, are not part of all this
but you can be part of the reason why crime is not any worse
than it is.
We see houses being broken into and people being mugged
on a regular basis.
In 1963, Martin Luther King had a dream.
And today I have a dream.
I dream of a better world without crime.
Without drugs or pointless killing.
A world without injustice and racism.
Where everyone is equal and no one is forced to live on the streets.
Of course, this is just a dream,
and I am sure that you, too, have once dreamt so;
But if you just make that small effort to donate whatever small
change you have, or whatever old sheets you do no longer want,
it may not seem like very much but you could be making
a huge difference.

Jerome Wren (13)
Lycée Francais Charles de Gaulle, London

I Have A Dream

You are judged these days,
On whether you are black or white.
By making this prejudgement,
You are putting irony in the sentence:
'Don't judge a book by its cover',
Because it is, most importantly,
The inside that counts,
That defines you as a human being.
In the end, we are all the same,
Born on the same planet,
Living the same lives.
There is no group out-performing the other
Because intelligence is determined by yourself,
By your brain and your way of thinking.
Take, for example, a convenience store:
The outside can be classy, modern and attractive,
But what you're really looking for is,
As the name suggests,
Its convenience, its practicality
And its ability to make you find what you want.
It is the same with human beings,
The outside can make you judge
A person too quickly,
Because it is, in the end, with the inner being
You will get along with.

Nicolas Hall (13)
Lycée Francais Charles de Gaulle, London

The Essential

1961, Berlin's wall was there
1989, a big blank space
Could anything be as easy
But in less time
Than this 28 dreadful years of pain?
Martin Luther King had a dream
We all have one
But what is it exactly?
No more drugs, no more racism or death penalty?
This would be good for humanity
But is it the most importrant?
What is worth the happiness of a family?
What is worth the love of sisters and brothers?

1929, World War II had started
1945, hopefully, nothing more to say
Could anything be as easy
But in less time
Than these 6 years of death?
All humans are the same:
2056, we wish to be young
1996, we wish to be old
In these 60 years our thoughts have changed
But did our love change?
All humans are the same:
We sometimes hope that hours are minutes
Or some day, that minutes are hours

But I hope
That humans will always remember what is, for them
'The essential'.

Pierre-Edouard Altieri (13)
Lycée Francais Charles de Gaulle, London

I Have A Dream

Is there a world
That doesn't involve war?
Is there a world
That only involves peace?

Is there a place
Where birds sing?
Is there a place
Where the flowers come out in spring?

Maybe there's a planet
Where all the children come out to play
Maybe there's a place
Where people are *happy* all day

I hate the way
We all have to fight
And the fact
That some don't see the light

I have a dream
You probably have it too
But the question is
Will it ever come true?

Anastasia Kinsky (12)
Lycée Francais Charles de Gaulle, London

Loneliness

Loneliness
Is a terrible sadness.
No one should be alone
No one should be on their own.
Why don't we start making friends,
It would make everything so simple?
Schools would be better places
Only if we have what it takes
To get to know someone else
I believe friendliness is the key
To stop everyone from being lonely.
I believe that humanity has to see
That some people are lonely
And they need to be free and happy
To make that happen.
We all have to be friends,
I hope you understand
That this could be the end
Of what makes people sad.
The world doesn't have to be like that
We can make it change
But it won't be easy.
At least give it a try
It could be worth it.

Bideau Grégoire (13)
Lycée Francais Charles de Gaulle, London

War And Peace

Israel and Palestine
Two states at war
A war of crime
And hatred: a dreadful war.

Why is it so simple
To hate each other
When relations crumble
And cause disaster?

Take the Berlin Wall:
1961 it is built
1989 it falls
And Berliners still stand tall.

So maybe patience
Is the key
To all this intolerance
And cruelty.

Paul Jones (14)
Lycée Francais Charles de Gaulle, London

Why Should We Care?
It Is Not Our War

You're walking down the street,
You're full of hope, you have your sweets, you have your life.
You have everything you could ever want and ever need.
A truck passes by, filled with men
Their guns are shiny and new,
Their helmets glint in the hot summer sun.
Then the bullets fly, an explosion rocks the lovely new truck.
Men are everywhere, they scream and shout,
They scream in pain, in fear, in hate.
They are screaming, you are screaming.
The bullet wasn't meant for you, it wasn't meant for anyone
But it finds a mark, it finds a life to take away.
There is no pain, there is no fear
Just blood that stains your T-shirt.
Death has come to claim his reward,
In a dusty street on the other side of the world.

Alexander Davison (13)
Lycée Francais Charles de Gaulle, London

The Mess Of Colours

Red, yellow, green and blue,
Everybody sees things from a different view,
But what makes these colours,
What gives us light?
The two main colours,
Black and white.

Put together with brightness and dark,
These two pigments embraced,
Will give us a light to shine through the dark.

Then why do we still try,
To separate our world,
To live a lie,
To bring no colours in our words.

Why do we divide ourselves,
Why do we give less
To some who need more?
There is no answer to that mess,
There is no reason at all.

Calypso Varotsis (14)
Lycée Francais Charles de Gaulle, London

The Scarecrow

All day long he sits there working,
At eight, he comes home,
Has dinner and goes to bed.

A very simple man for the complex days he has.
He is a gentle, kind man,
But also an ignorant one too.

Throughout his life,
Never has he helped a suffering person,
Never has he tried to help end poverty,
Never has he tried to help end world hunger,
Never has he given a little to help a lot.

Not only does he ignore human beings
But also the environment.
Never has he recycled,
Nor has he ever fixed the polluting motor of his car,
This man has never done anything wrong;
He just watches and waits for things to happen
Like a scarecrow.

Aniort Simon (13)
Lycée Francais Charles de Gaulle, London

Welcome To Our World

The climate gets worse
We set our own curse
Destroying our Earth
One thousand die when another gives birth

Why nuclear powers?
The fault is all ours
Polluting our centres
Regretting ideas from the greatest inventors

Creating chemicals
Another idea stalls
We could make a change
A change that could be made by all

From doctors to engineers
From lawyers to volunteers
We're all born for a reason
Some are born to treason

We're here today
To change the world
And the display
A new day, a newborn, a new world.

Kevin Mamalis (13)
Lycée Francais Charles de Gaulle, London

Choices

'World' is a word linked to good and bad
Yet it means the same to both
'World' is a powerful word used to represent the people
But I realise now that it is wrongly applied
This world is meant to mean unity and indifference
Yet it does not, people are different
We choose our friends and our enemies
We love choices and opinions
We are not the same.

When people hear this word, they think what I thought
But what if we represent our surroundings by something else?
Such as a person, an object or even a feeling
What would it be?

It could be a sea of hate filled with fear
And all the good could fill a single river
This river faces death every day
How must it survive?

It could be a plain bush
And the good could come from that one rose.
This rose can barely stand on its own
How is it meant to fight?

What has the world been dominated by to this day?
Simple, war, hate and fear.

We have been reduced to obeying through fear.
We are afraid to give our opinions
Well, what if we did?
What if we said what we thought aloud?
Then maybe, just maybe, we could live in peace.

Astrid Van Campenhout (13)
Lycée Francais Charles de Gaulle, London

One Chance . . .

The time has come
we have the chance, this death charade is done.
We tried to kill this demon off,
we missed a chance to see.
We tried to fight our enemy
but he is you and he is me.

This world is ours,
we are to blame,
but hope it does remain.
We'll take it back from him.
A simple world, a loving world
all is yet to come.
The past must not haunt again.

Opportunity has come,
it will not stay.
Put down your sword,
take up your world
into your own hands.
Demand the truth,
hold on to hope,
he will leave us soon.

We have tried,
We have failed,
and yet we must move on.
The time has come,
we have the chance . . .

Elisabeth Brown (14)
Lycée Francais Charles de Gaulle, London

I Have A Dream

I have a dream,
Where the world is at peace.
Could it actually happen?
The world must be appeased.
I must end the pain,
End the famine,
So we can be happy again,
On this sad, lonely planet.

I have a hope,
That the world could be cleansed of oppositions,
Because war puts thousands in tough positions.
Our planet and all on it need aid,
Why can't Man keep the world the way it was made?
It is a sad, sad thing to see the world now,
I must help change it, but I wonder how.

I have a fear,
I don't see how we can be helped at all,
I've tried and tried but they just won't hear my call.
I hate the state of our planet now,
I must do something to help but how?
I don't know, I don't care, I must think of something,
I must find a way to end the rebellion, fighting, kicking and punching.

I am scared . . .

Daniel Weiser (12)
Lyndhurst House Preparatory School, London

You Only Get One Life

I wish there was no war, crime or terrorism.
There is too much hatred in the world today.
Albert Einstein, Michelangelo, Leonardo Da Vinci,
Great men who have changed the world.
Virtues and hope are what we should strive for,
There will be the temptation to do wrong,
But always stop and think.
Annihilation and war sway us from our beliefs.
Years and years ago Hitler swayed people,
Remember forever who you are and what you believe in.
Always follow your dream,
One person can change millions of lives.
Life must be lived
For the best, to the full,
The loss of a dad, scarred me very deeply,
You have only one life,
Now live it, you matter.

Nathaniel Greenwold (11)
Lyndhurst House Preparatory School, London

Chipping Away

In my sleep I dream of being
a footballer or a superstar
I'm a boy
But sometimes I dream of a better world
I know there is no good without evil
No hero without a villain
But if we chip away at the wall of negativity
It will tumble
But if we don't we will never see what's on the other side
All the little things we do
All the little chips
Add up.

Jamie Elwes (12)
Lyndhurst House Preparatory School, London

Without A Care

I have a dream that I can soar like a bird,
Without fear of death and starvation,
Without worrying about the world,
And stop the annihilation of God's creation.

I have a dream that I can glide like a swan,
Without fear of evil,
Without fear that the sun will go,
And leave the world to die and kill.

I have a dream that I can dance like a butterfly,
In a world where we all share,
Where we would all be one family,
So I could soar, glide and dance without a care.

Liam Biser (11)
Lyndhurst House Preparatory School, London

Global Warming

When a car uses fuel, I know what happens; I cannot
lie to myself, but as my selfless acts grow older every
day, I doubt if I can still make a difference.

When the greenhouse effect gets worse I know it's
partly my fault.

I know there will be a tomorrow, but if I don't start to
improve, I will be filled with sorrow

As I walk through this world, two roads diverge into a
fumed street, I wonder what the future holds, if
there is a future that is.

It is clear now that I have made the wrong choice and
that has made all the difference.

Ross Grier (12)
Salesian College, Farnborough

Truth

Stereotyping,
A mistake we all make;
The young are dangerous, the old weak and miserable,
That's what people see us as,
But those who show the world the truth,
Are the real heroes.
We stand around, hoping for peace,
Governments ruling our lives.
And all of us make no difference,
If just one person would show their true colours,
The whole world would follow in their wake.
I go into a shop but get dismissed straight away,
I wouldn't take anything, I don't cause trouble,
Why do people view me like this?
Stand up, be strong!
Show everyone what you are really like,
Then equality would be spread
And stereotypes wouldn't judge us
For what we aren't.

Alex Semper-White (13)
Salesian College, Farnborough

It Spares No One And Everyone

I wish, I wish to break through the dark,
The hope, the despair.
I wish, I wish to destroy the anger,
Which kills the world.

I wish, I wish that they could stop,
The heartless fire burning all.
I wish, I wish the light would prevail,
And destroy the terror left inside.

I wish, I wish the darkness to stop,
To keep children for the future.
I wish, I wish it was now nothing,
I wish, I wish terrorism would kill no more.

Justin Hobbs (13)
Salesian College, Farnborough

Heatwave

You thought today was hot,
But what comes tomorrow,
You decide.

You thought today was hot,
But tomorrow will be hotter,
If we continue our ways.

You thought today was hot,
But with all the cars being,
What could you expect?

You thought today was hot,
Take your bike to work,
It will help those summer days
To stay as they are at the moment.

You thought today was hot,
Help the planet today,
What has it ever done to you?

You thought today was hot,
But what comes tomorrow?
You decide.

Jonathan Clarke (13)
Salesian College, Farnborough

Baby In A Chair

Like a baby in a chair,
I live in a country,
Where the government control,
My future and my every move,
I do nothing for myself,
Everything is provided,
A nanny, looking after a helpless infant.

The dictators rule by force,
By massacres and murders,
However, our politicians rule by lies,
They don't need fear,
The lie that the people have control is enough.
Spin doctors doctor the story,
Secretaries hide information,
And leaders lead the way,
All we do is listen and follow.

There is another way,
We can have the choice,
We can make our own decisions,
Force a proper system of democracy,
Not the lies we are being fed now,
Then we shall grow up,
Gain control of our futures,
Move out of the chair and stand up,
This is the true freedom of democracy.

Jamie Pelling (13)
Salesian College, Farnborough

The Choices

Our lives controlled by the government,
Our young men sent to a pointless war,
The sky, a mass of choking black smoke,
The trenches flooded, water dropping every second,
Trench flooded, water dropping every second,
Trench foot seeks for a soldier or two,
The death toll continually rising,
Just think.

Listen to the racist comments,
On the football pitches and on the streets,
Whether you're black,
Or white, don't fight,
Think back to Martin Luther King,
A leader to peace,
Just think.

Watch as global warming changes the world,
Temperature, water levels, water temperatures,
Torrential rain and storms,
Vegetation eventually struggling to grow,
Animals and humans dying from heatstroke,
Just stand, and think about what you are doing,
The choices you should make.

We can change the future if we try,
A better life for the next generations,
Thinking about the future.

Nicholas Stayt (12)
Salesian College, Farnborough

A Peaceful World

Will tomorrow ever come?
A world without fighting and war.
A world without guns and grenades.
A world without death and destruction.
Will this nightmare ever end?
The night we call human life.
Can't we just be peaceful and cease the fighting,
Shake hands and call a truce?
The ball is in our court now,
Why sink to their level and return the shot.
Throw a bomb into their court and watch the bodies fall.
Children watch their parents struggle
As they are forced to leave their homes.
They are the true prisoners of *war.*
Can't we just be peaceful and cease the fighting!

Connor Jackson (13)
Salesian College, Farnborough

Two Communities

Is this a fair world?
Black being in sorrow,
White being in happiness,
Two different races; but mostly similar,
Both in one world,
Both in one world,
Refusing to join into the one community,
There is only one ruler in this place,
Inequality,
But that can change,
But that can change,
Equality between black and white will rule some day,
It will rule some day,
People will realise that this is the only way,
The only way.

Nosherwaan Mahmood (13)
Salesian College, Farnborough

There Will Be A Tomorrow?

'Go on Charles,
Everyone else has had one.'
I reach for the packet,
My hand is shaking,
I grab one,
Stick it in my mouth
And light it up.
Suddenly a terrible taste,
My mind says it's delicious,
Like 1,000 sweet things all at once.
I start coughing,
Why did I want to talk to these people?
I just want to go home and smoke.
'I'll be seeing you, later.'
I walk home and buy three packets of cigarettes,
I said they were for my mum.
Two weeks now after my first,
Now my insides hurt.
Light, then darkness.
Next thing I know I'm in a bed.
'I am afraid he has lung cancer, has he been smoking?'
The voices sound so far away.
'Of course not, he's only 15,' I hear my mother say.
'Mum,' I try to speak, it's so hard, 'Mum, I have been smoking.
'Mum, I try to raise an arm. I can't.
'Mum,' it was the first word I ever said and the last.
Many weeks later,
Before smoking takes its toll.

Adam Perryman (13)
Salesian College, Farnborough

Ticking Time Bomb

To dream or not to dream. That is the question,
Whether to leave the future as it is
And let the world destroy itself
Or change the present,
And make the future look bright.
The question that occurred in people's minds.
Martin Luther King, Nelson Mandela,
Changed the present for us.
Now we should change the future
For those who live it.

Now we have to take responsibility,
You and I, change the world,
Get rid of racism and poverty.
Not for being famous,
But to change the future.

The ball is in our court now,
We have to reply before time runs out.
To dream, to do, to take action,
That is what we should do.

Lewis McIlroy (13)
Salesian College, Farnborough

What

(Based on 'Man is what he believes' Anton Chekhov)

What shall the world become
If the foundations of our society
Are frail and weak
If the ideals we base our lives on
Are twisted and wrong
If we never learn from our mistakes
If we don't listen to each other
If we forget to care
If racism prevails
What shall the world become?

George Keenan (13)
Salesian College, Farnborough

Am I A Waste Of Space?

I am fed up,
They've been doing it for days,
Will the teachers ever notice,
The name-calling in the playground,
Or do their tea and biscuits have the priority?

They tell me I'm a mistake,
A waste of space,
I've never heard the words, 'I love you.'
Will they grow out of it?
Will I ever be popular?

I've tried to be cool,
But I'm awful at football,
The girls say I'm ugly,
The boys say I'm a geek.

So I was a mistake,
A waste of space,
The girls say I'm a geek,
But my mum says I'm cool!

Simon Tudor (13)
Salesian College, Farnborough

A Chance To Save

People fear change,
For many different reasons.
Fear.
Fear of the unknown and diversity.

We have a chance to save,
A chance to save the future.
People in the past have tried,
Martin Luther King,
Oscar Romero.

They all had dreams,
But died because of them.
The people that killed them were like hungry dogs,
Always looking for their lives.

What has become of this world?
Not many people care,
Of what others try to do,
But some are brave enough to dare.

Jim Sanderson (13)
Salesian College, Farnborough

To Dream Or Not To Dream

To dream or not to dream, that is the question.
To dream of changing future minds.
To stand against treacherous lies from twisted minds.
To defeat the beasts where in society they lie.
And by doing free whole communities of prejudicial ties.
By acting to say we end
The pain and the struggle of some lives forced by others.
It's a large dilemma. Not to be wished. To dream and act
Or watch and ignore, not work just relax. Yes, there's the itch.
For in work what do I gain? Pride? Respect? Self-fulfilment?
If I laze and watch to the end.
What guilt would I feel, what shame at myself?
That maketh conscience my dilemma.
For who would bear the shame of letting weakness cloud
Thy judgement?
It is the good man's failing.
For he watched and did not act.
Those who had stood strong would shun him.
Who had rebelled against wrong. He would be the outcast.
When work must be done to help those in pain.
When with needle must burdens be born.
To grunt and sweat in bittersweet defiance
But to watch and relax is so tempting. To watch time be sliced away.
That easy joy, from those who wait
Few return to the harder life.
The nectar that makes us prefer guilt to pain and pride.
To not do the work that mocks and laughs,
To watch and wait for events to unfold.
But what happens if it goes wrong when I haven't dreamed,
Haven't acted.
That's why I have to dream to force myself into action.
The power of dreams is to create hope and with hope
Comes better change.

Alexander Rhodes (13)
Salesian College, Farnborough

What Goes On In London Square?

You see them lying in the street,
But do you ever think.
Where they live and what they eat,
When sleeping in the cold.

You do not notice them,
You walk by when you see them,
They ask for money,
But they're stuck in London Square.

Why leave them out,
They've done nothing wrong,
It isn't their fault they're there.

Give them shelter,
Give them food,
Give them what they need.

A loving family,
Out of the cold,
Where good things happen at last.

Soon they're gone,
In families that care,
They are finally loved and cared for.

The sadness sleeps,
But for how long,
Depends how we keep you.

John Blackwood (13)
Salesian College, Farnborough

Why Shouldn't The World

It doesn't matter what colour you are,
We must all be friends and respect each other,
Don't label people,
Or assume they do wrong.

Don't be unfair, accept different ideas,
We all have rights and nobody should be left out,
Fighting isn't an issue,
And peace should be made.

No differences and conflict between us,
We live in a mixed race society,
We exist together,
We should all be friends.

It doesn't matter about your culture,
It all adds to the colourful world
The fighting should stop,
Sport has kicked racism out - why shouldn't the world?

Ross MacSwan (13)
Salesian College, Farnborough

Play The Game Fair And Square

The world may have its problems but corruption is the worst in
my eyes,
If one man in this world can resist against being bribed, then the whole
world will follow on,
However much he is tempted he will always be loyal to his ways of life.
Some people will knock him down for doing the right thing in life.
He knows though that if he keeps going he will make a real success of
the world.
It matches up with the Chinese proverb, 'If you give a man a fish he'll
eat for a day but if you teach him to fish he'll eat for a lifetime'.
Corruption shall be stopped if one man's dream can come true.

Nicholas Roberts (12)
Salesian College, Farnborough

Society's Wallet

Spare change.
While you ride around buying yourself satisfaction,
You don't take your change,
You throw us onto the floor, because
We weigh you down.
We aren't shiny,
We're not important.
You turn a blind eye because
We're nearly worth worthless.
I laugh at your self centredness.
We're piling up, sooner or later,
You will have to pick us up.
Pick me up
And keep me.
A small thing can make
A big difference.

Michael Ayiotis (13)
Salesian College, Farnborough

Stop The Suffering

Screams everywhere,
Smoke coming from the scene,
Scrap metal.
The whole world in panic.
Lives lost.
Police everywhere,
Ambulances everywhere,
Fire engines everywhere.
The worst form of murder possible,
Mourned by thousands.
Suicide, murder, suffering all under one roof.
Governments being criticised,
All the world suffers.
It has to stop.
Now.

Joshua Pallett (13)
Salesian College, Farnborough

Colours of People's Skin

Black and white skin
English and African
People are discriminated
Because of these things

This is not fair
They can change
These facts of life
What does it matter
What colour skin you have?

No one cares about
The colour eyes and
Hair you have
So why is the skin and
Country different?

People deserve these
Basic human rights
They can't be denied
This freedom of life.

Zachary Moore (12)
Salesian College, Farnborough

Death Beheld

There will be a tomorrow,
But full of morning sorrow,
People will die, their bodies destroyed,
Their families' hope thrown to the void,
Stripped of rights, tortured till death,
Kicked, punched, blocked from breath.

Is this what life provides?
With terror, despair and many divides,
Is this what the future will hold?
Hope lost, pain induced, cold, oh so cold.

Scarcely given bread and water,
Until the people come and slaughter,
Life is torn from bodies many
People worth just a single penny.

Rufus Driscoll (13)
Salesian College, Farnborough

Angry At The World

I'm angry that the government of today,
Won't pay to let us see some more Mays.
I'm angry that the law right now,
Lets paedophiles, rapists, murders and terrorists,
Get away with so many fouls.
I'm angry that, while people grow fat,
People are dying, from the other facts,
How they can't afford a roof to save them from the rain,
And that their own governments cause them pain.
I'm angry that people work so hard
To earn less than a pound of lard.
I'm angry how much money you can get from kicking a football,
Whereas people work the whole week and have to sleep in a
Charity hall.
I'm angry that whilst people are crying from a scraped knee,
People are dying from an unknown disease.
I'm angry that whilst I'm writing this poem
All these bad things keep on going.

Courtney Walsh (13)
Salesian College, Farnborough

Freedom Is Golden

Terror kept me from feeling safe,
Men lost their lives for noble reasons.
However motives should have never been brought up
And men that died should still be.

I'm waiting for you,
You being the day that everyone
Grown-up or child can feel safe,
Safe in the knowledge of no terror.

There will be a tomorrow when everyone is equal,
No black or white, religion doesn't matter.
Everyone as equals will feel secure,
And fighting will cease.

People killing, people dying,
The way they die is not with pride but anger.
Blown to bits or fearing the worst,
Innocents are still killed,
Governments argue
And citizens bear the brunt of contention.

Chris Chianalino (13)
Salesian College, Farnborough

There's Always Tomorrow

Where I come from,
What I think doesn't count.
Fifty million different views,
You can see why.
What annoys me most though,
Is when a million agree,
And still, no one listens.
Democratic country?
I don't think so.
Our views don't count.
We're told what to do.
Led by lies.
But still we mustn't give in,
Eventually they will have to listen.
'The more, the better'
As some would say.
So don't give up,
There's always tomorrow.

Tom Dodington (13)
Salesian College, Farnborough

Silent Suspicion

It is so easy to blame me,
For all the wrongs in the world.
Your world,
Where everything goes wrong,
And you get angry,
I always take the blame.
It is not fair,
You shout at me,
I never answer,
I'm suddenly on the ground.
But I never retaliate,
You have everything,
I have nothing.
Just because I am a child,
It does not mean that it does not hurt,
People hear,
Nobody knows,
But everyone suspects.

Archie Shortland (13)
Salesian College, Farnborough

Light Or Dark?

Colour can be the best creation ever,
Though it can be cruelly twisted.
It can make your room welcoming
It can segregate you from others.

Colour should only result in compliments
All over the Earth insults can occur
Less frequent are the compliments
Tragically, more insults are found.

There is a whole spectrum of colour to choose from
Only two affect us in everyday life.
Fashion designers slave to make great colour
Others became slaves because of it.

If we all agree colour does not affect us
We could achieve what no other has done
Though improbable it could occur,
That colour really does not matter.

Jordan Ainslie (13)
Salesian College, Farnborough

Why Do They Smoke

Will there be a tomorrow?
The death dealing clouds,
Rise from their mouths,
Their deaths drawing ever closer.
Will there be a tomorrow for them?

Why do they do it?
Each rotten life-sapping stick.
They jam between their yellow lips,
Sapping their lives away.
Why do they do it? Why?

What do they get?
An early death,
A painful death,
One more grave beneath the stars.
What do they get?
Just death.

Robert Guy (13)
Salesian College, Farnborough

Needle And Thread

Never may our world be sewn back together,
As it is slowly and painfully being torn apart,
By war and death.
Death of old and young
Precious life wasted.

I wish the wars would stop,
The anger felt by all, drained away
The destruction prevented
Weapons dropped
I wish, I wish, I wish for all world peace.

I wish that words spoken would bring a smile to faces,
And will not make anyone angry or upset
The actions that we do,
Will not harm or offend,
But be actions of sharing and peace.

I wish all of this so that,
One day one of our children or their children
Will not prick themselves on a needle,
As they try to sew the world back together.

Alex Cave (13)
Salesian College, Farnborough

Amakuru (Outcast)

World's on fire . . . ?

Avalanches of red clouds draw near.
Carving hollow holes;
With burning stars falling endlessly.

White actions, the enemy of thought
The friend of illusions,
The crook of raceless faces.
Amakuru?

Cherished freedom,
From a deathless era;
When blight, blinding white light
Is mastering the world
In the silent dark.

Amakuru
Frowns . . . a smile . . . ?
Frown . . . smiles . . . ?

The dark month arises,
And there right over there . . . subliminal hate
pierces through;
Breathing in the infinite deceptions,
Feeding on the discriminations.

Yearned personhood:
Easy to digest
Hard to swallow.

Delusional peace, clouds their mind
Land for all . . . ?
Peace for all . . . ?

Fiona Habiyambere (16)
Selsdon High School, South Croydon

I Have A Dream

Emptiness fills me,
Nothing fills him.
Tears are in my eyes,
But he still feels nothing.
I pray and pray wide awake at night,
His eyes are shut, his hand is cold,
He is gone.

I had a dream where worry nor fear could be felt,
A dream where blood did not pour nor did it spill.
A dream where all the suffering stopped,
A dream where death was peaceful and painless.

I had a dream that the Earth was free of disease.

Cecilie Tett
The Harrodian School, London

The Adventures With Peter Pan

Come to my window,
Hold my hand,
Take me away to Neverland.

We'll fly over London, past Big Ben,
By the time we get there, it will be morning.
The feeling of flying is ever so light,
If you don't like heights it would give you a fright.

We'll swim with the mermaids, play with the sprites,
Dance with the Indians and fight the pirates,
Run from the crocodile with a clock in his belly,
Whenever Hook hears him, his legs turn to jelly.

We'll play, we'll dance, we'll fight, we'll fly,
But watch out for Hook, he's every so sly.
Hook put poison in your drink,
You didn't drink it, instead it was Tink.

He hit your forehead with his hook,
You're covered in blood, I don't want to look.
But I couldn't leave you with something you'll miss,
So I bent over and gave you a kiss.

Come to my window,
Hold Jane's hand,
Take her away to Neverland.

Sherrilee Burnett (13)
The Sholing Technology College, Sholing

I Have A Dream

Crying, cuts, bruises, guts
It's wrong
Not when I get really badly hurt
And treated like dirt
It's wrong

Confidence knocked
Childhood blocked
Whatever my age
Please cool down the temperature gauge
Take a walk, punch a pillow
But please don't take your anger out on me

I hurt, I bleed
I'm not a punchbag on a lead
Please don't hurt me
I beg, I plead

Your fists are like bombs on my already battered face
I wish, I wish I could get out of this place
I may be small
And not so tall
But I talk and live
And all you have to give
Is punching, kicks
Breaking me into bits
Snapping parts of me in half
Then you stand by my side and laugh

I have a dream
It's a wonderful dream of a safer place, a haven
Where my face is whole and no blood drips from me
Where I'm loved, not hated
Where I really am appreciated
For just being me

I'm treated with love and care
And where no one dares to hurt me
Remember I have a dream too
It's not just you.

Mia Keens (12)
The Toynbee School, Eastleigh